i

Divine Order
For
Spiritual Dominance

Dr. Paula A. Price
D.Min., Ph.D.

Flaming Vision Publications
Tulsa, Oklahoma

Revised Edition

© 2005 by Dr. Paula A. Price

Unless otherwise indicated, all scriptural quotations are from the *King James Version* of the Bible.

Divine Order for Spiritual Dominance

Flaming Vision Publications

Tulsa, Oklahoma 74136

ISBN 1-886288-11-9

Table of Contents

CHAPTER ONE   **2**

The Difference Between 1 Corinthians 12:28, 29 & Ephesians 4:11   2

Eternity Decrees Spirit of Corinthians   4

God's Divine Order Imposed on the Church   5

A Practical Exercise Visualizes Five-Fold Significance   6

The Evangelist   8

The Pastor   9

The Teacher   10

Apostles & Prophets   11

Another Problem with Modern Five-Fold Views   13

Five-Fold or...   14

Two Mantles that Did Not Contribute to the New Testament   15

CHAPTER TWO   **17**

The Importance of Titles   18

Classic Definitions of a Minister   18

What is a Title?   23

Defining a Title   25

About Authority   26

Titles Began Divine   27

Titles Back in Time   27

Founding an Institution   28

Officers Staff Institutions   30

Traditional Church View of Titles   30

Titles Do Not Infect Hearts   32

What Comes From Within Defiles   32

Suggested Activity   35

CHAPTER THREE   **37**

Applying the Term Five-Fold to Christian Ministry   38

The Five-Fold Hand Analogy in Scripture   38

The Bible's Hand Imagery   39

Role and Goal of the Five-Fold Officers   40

God's Holy Scriptures Equate to Eternity's Constitutional Government of Earth   41

The Ministry Is Christ's   45

What Christ's Ministry Consists Of   45

E-4 Ministry Holds No Personal Prerogatives   46

About The Eleven Descriptives   48

The Minimal Staff of the New Testament Church   49

23 Practical Reasons for the Five-Fold   50

God's Spiritual Equipment for Ministry Service   51

Know Your Work Chart   54

CHAPTER FOUR   **55**

Public Office, Private Devotions, Public Ministry   56

Theology & Doctrine   58

A God View of the Church's Offices   61

God's Kingdom is Spirit   62

The Ecclesia   63

Confirming Ecclesiastical Citizenship   66

CHAPTER FIVE   **68**

The Bible's Premise: Eternity in the Now   72

Jesus' Doctrine from Heaven   74

Our Best Sin's Rest   75

Human Brilliance Compensates for Sin Condition   77

Archaic Struggles with Sin's Grip   80

Human Worship from Adam to Christ   80

CHAPTER SIX   **82**

Gifts unto Men: The Kind of Gifts Christ Gave   83

The Gift is an Officer   85

The Meaning of an Officer   85

The Weight of an Office   86

46 Five-Fold Duties   87

Describing an Office   93

Why Offices Persist   95

CHAPTER SEVEN   **97**

Creation Manifests Divine Order   *98*

Creator Design Limits Arbitrary Ministry   *103*

Ministry & Minister: A General Survey   *105*

A Biblical Concept of Official Divine Service   *107*

How the Human Divine Relationship Began   *107*

The Ministry from the Priest's Office   *108*

Biblical Terms Depict an Office   *110*

Divine Office Applied   *111*

CHAPTER EIGHT   **113**

Problem of No or Poor Office Criteria   *115*

Bible Examples of Criteria   *117*

Table of Officers & Offices   *118*

God's Old Testament Pattern   *121*

Human Instincts Insufficient for Office Recognition   *122*

Officer Features & Office Functions   *124*

Differing Outcomes Require Different Objectives   *125*

CHAPTER NINE   **127**

The Anointing's Apothecary   *128*

The Anointing is a Resource and a Person   *129*

Dispensation and the Anointing   *130*

Dispensation Means Economy   *130*

The Anointing's Two-Tiered Dispensation   *131*

How Chrio Differs   *136*

CHAPTER TEN   **137**

How Important are Signs?   *138*

Signs Also Served Prophecy   *139*

The Bible & Miracles   *140*

Prophecy as a Miracle   *143*

Wonders   *143*

The Ministry of the Dunamite   *144*

CHAPTER ELEVEN   **146**

Deciding on the Right Covering   *147*

What Is a Covering?   148
The Covering Tree   149
Determining Your Best Covering   150
The Need for Mentorship   152
Considerations for a Covering Relationship   153
Forming Covering Unions   153
Choosing Influence Rather Than Control   154
Motivations for Spiritual Covering   154
Lesser Better, Stronger Weaker Questions   156
Guidelines for Spiritual Coverers   157
CHAPTER TWELVE   **159**
History of the Tithe?   160
The Rightful Recipient of the Tithe   160
The Melchizedek Tithe   161
Understanding the Ancient Temple   163
Spiritual Covering & the Tithe   164
CHAPTER THIRTEEN   **166**
A Biblical Model for Spiritual Coverings   167
Quality Spiritual Covering Protocols   167
Staffing Protocols   168
Tithing Protocols   168
CHAPTER FOURTEEN   **170**
Traditional Mentorship Formation   171
Indicators of a Promising Mentorship   173
Critical Requirements of Suitable Mentors   173
Indicators of an Unstable Mentorship Mix   174
Mentoree Duties: Coming Under Your Mentor's Wing   176
Glossary of Key Terms   **178**
Table of Sources & References   **185**

Preface

We appreciate your purchase and use of our materials and pray God's richest blessings of enlightenment education upon you as you enjoy *"Divine Order for Spiritual Dominance."* As this work is a combination teaching and study guide, it is understood that your new book will be generally used for your personal study and development. However, if you are a member of the Ephesians 4:11 staff of the New Testament church, you will be doubly blessed to find it also makes an excellent teaching tool for this all-important subject in your church, school, or staff of ministers.

Comprehensive in nature, as with most of our academic publications, this book too includes lessons, planning guides, lecture outlines, assignments and casework, practicum, and reviews for the teacher, likely in a separate teacher text. Collectively, these resources comprise the elements of a curriculum and are why our texts frequently find themselves in group studies, classrooms, schools, seminars, and workshops. To assure proper regard is given the author for the material, the publisher gives no permission for any reader or user to reproduce, resale, transmit or distribute this book in whole or in part without written authorization first from the author and/or the publisher. Should the intended use of this work be as a supplement or complement to an existing curriculum or as a lone course, written permission from the publisher is also necessary before distributing its learning and teaching aids, and/or formally teaching it to students.

Whenever the subject matter contained in this book is taught or referred to publicly, proper recognition and acknowledgment of its author and title are required to assure due credit for the work is given to its originator. The same applies to significant excerpts taken from the book for use in other writings. A written release for such use must first be secured from the publisher.

If you are interested in enjoying the benefits, privileges, and discounts of being an Everlasting Life Education Network member, contact the publisher at the address below:

Flaming Vision Publications, 7030 C. S. Lewis Avenue, #468,

Tulsa, OK 74136

CHAPTER ONE
A Subject Seminar

Chapter Topics:

The Difference Between 1 Corinthians 12:28,29 & Ephesians 4:11 •
Eternity Decrees Spirit of Corinthians "Set" Apostles, Prophets,
Teachers • God's Divine Order Imposed on the Church •

A Practical Exercise Visualizes Five-Fold Significance • Another
Problem with Modern Five-Fold Views • Five-Fold Or... • Two
Mantles that Did Not Contribute to the New Testament

Before extensively tackling the Ephesians 4:11 subject, one must ask why the question is hardly ever addressed in the context of those listed in 1 Corinthians 12:28, 29. It seems when the church's offices are discussed one or the other, is given more attention. The five fold is usually addressed more than the Corinthian headship. However, if no other scripture settles the argument about God's intended order, apostles and prophets in particular, this one does.

The Difference Between 1 Corinthians 12:28, 29 & Ephesians 4:11

That the Ephesians 4:11 list was penned five to ten years after the Corinthians reference is significant. It could be that the church's growth compelled the emergence of the evangelist and pastor as standing functions in the church. As it spread and settled in the world Paul's re-articulation of the church's leadership became necessary. In the 1 Corinthians 12:28, 29 list, God set (appointed, ordained, installed) first apostles, second prophets and third teachers. This wording differs from that of Ephesians 4:11 where it says He (Christ) **gave** (presented, granted, bestowed, provided) some (with) apostles, prophets, evangelists, pastors and teachers. In the last instance, a bestowed gift as opposed to an ordained appointment draws the dividing line. Of the many synonymic meanings[1] of the term, installation, appointment, and ordination are some. To install someone is to inaugurate them, invest them with power and instate or induct them into office.

In about the mid twelfth century the word *ordain* was understood to mean *assign, decree, appoint, arrange*, and *order*. The idea was that those ordained were assigned to put in order by appointment. In exploring the word "set" used in the Corinthians reference, research says it means:

- To fix firmly in place before the end of the first century
- Seated in a particular sequence
- A retinue; that is a following
- A sect

  (Note: The word *sect* identifies a religious order or body, a following such as that of a school of thought, as an example.)

From the above terms, it appears the translator of the passage well understood what the Lord led Paul to write centuries earlier, and that it pertained to what was yet flourishing at the time of the translation. That is God's official church appointments. The word *seated* shows up in the epistle to the Ephesians where the church is said to be, *seated* in Christ (Ephesians 1:3). Christ, on the other hand, is *set* at the Father's right hand in Ephesians 1:20, and His church co-seated with Him in heavenly places. Interestingly, Jesus' words in Matthew 19:28 imply more authority is commuted to the Corinthians positions than is imagined today: "*And Jesus said unto them, Verily I say unto you, That ye which have followed me, in the regeneration when the Son of man shall sit in the throne of his glory, ye also shall sit upon twelve thrones, judging the twelve tribes of Israel.*" See also Luke 22:14, 24, and 28-30: "*And when the hour was come, he sat down and the twelve*

---

[1] The Barnhart Concise Diction of Etymology: The Origins of American English Words; Robert Barnhart.

apostles with him…"; "And there was also a strife among them, which of them should be accounted the greatest…"; "Ye are they which have continued with me in my temptations. And I appoint unto you a kingdom, as my Father hath appointed unto me; that ye may eat and drink at my table in my kingdom, and sit on thrones judging the twelve tribes of Israel." Revelation 21:14 shows the Lord's word is already fulfilled at the end of the age.

The Ephesians 4:11 bestowals are dealing with the gifts that Christ gave to men, not the ordained installation of an official that the Corinthians reference underscores. Gifts are far from what the words "ordained" or "preordained" convey that include:

- Pre-destiny
- Divine Decree
- Predetermination
- Divine Order
- Intentional Designed
- Preordained
- Pre-appointed
- Fated

Eternity Decrees Spirit of Corinthians "Set" Apostles, Prophets, Teachers

These are all terms that have little to do with gifts, bestowal, endowment or anything of the kind. The prefix *pre-* in front of some of them speaks to sovereignty as the Creator's prerogative and perpetual will. The prefix *pre-* means "beforehand, in front of, ahead in place and rank or time." That on its own says a great deal. Hence, words beginning with it to vary a word aim to communicate the word's action as having be decreed or resolved beforehand, or that its object is ahead of others in its class in position, status and rank or time. In Bible eras, scribes who knew they were representatives of their deities or their religions were careful to note when their words conveyed in time our out of time events. Thus, words like predestined, preordained, preappointed, and predetermined served as common verbiage for writers of sacred texts. Knowing it was important to distinguish the immortality of their deities and the temporality of humanity, they consistently reminded their readers that their words predated their entrance into the world and would outlive them. Predestined for instance in the late thirteenth century came from a French term meaning "appointed or determined beforehand." By the next century, it was understood to mean, "foreordained by decree or purpose of God."

God ordained and Christ gave some to be or gave to some as ministry gifts in the bestowal more than presentation sense. Thus we may conclude that the Father God ordained three minimal offices to be occupied in His church as long as it remains on earth. Based on that Creator ordination, Jesus Christ upon succeeding in His redemptive mission gave, that is distributed, God's ordained offices to specific people groups in His body with one variation. He added the evangelist and pastor to the staff between the prophet and the teacher, leaving untouched what the Holy Spirit gave Paul in 1 Corinthians 12. This information should be considered when addressing the subject of God's five fold ministries to answer the question of why the Lord did not lead Paul to alter the position and implied status of the apostle and prophet and what transpired in the church's development that necessitated the pastor and evangelist he ignored in his divine appointments.

God's Divine Order Imposed on the Church

One hard to miss reality at present is that the Lord's compelling reorganization of His New Creation church into His divine order. Suddenly, articles, sermons, books and other media are tackling the subject are appearing everywhere. As the process goes on, questions and concerns arise about the church's restructure and beg for responsible and logical answers. When it comes to the five-fold, the primary question is, "What did *God* want His church to look like over time and how should it be structured to serve His ends?" Other questions and concerns include, "Why is Ephesians 4:11' staff of five ministers so important to Him? What exactly is the divine order it is claimed they represent? How may the church be structured according to scripture patterns and standards that least upsets established leaders and churches? How did the church get this way in the first place, and where do we begin the massive project of restoring the church to God's divine order?" Of course, the questions go on and here we concentrate on most of these as primary five-fold officer concerns. As we start out, the major question of them all today is that of God's sovereign move to impose this restoration on His church's organization after centuries of humanist disorder.

Significant in the church's present disorder is the absence of Christ's apostles and prophets, the founding officers of the church. God's restoration initiatives have already disturbed some church leaders and confused some of its members as well. Of great concern to the Lord, and His restored apostles and prophets, is the dearth of wisdom and knowledge available on the offices' mantles. The void may be blamed for the detrimental consequences to Christianity and the world. Up to late, the Christian church only had the ministries of the evangelist to the teacher to rely on in its rediscovery of what Jesus intended His church to look like and how He ordained it to operate. That the Spirit-filled church is classified as evangelical and sometimes evangelical fundamentalist establishes this truth. Besides this is the erroneous labeling of the fourth member of the Ephesians 4:11 staff, the pastor, as the New Testament church's primary head, for which there exists no biblical precedence or scripture pattern in the New Testament.

So widely accepted is the misconception that schools, Bible colleges, and Christian universities all blindly endorse it. Various church and para-church organizations institutionalized the glaring mistake to give it the perceived power of New Testament canon that it apparently holds today in many religious camps: The pastor heads the church locally and globally—period. To see how ingrained this belief is read many of the books that quote the five-fold and you will see quite often the list goes like this: *apostle, prophet, pastor, evangelist, and teacher;* instead of how it really reads in Ephesians 4:11: "apostles, prophets, evangelists, pastors, and teachers." The pastor is way down the line, actually number four on the staff. With a misprint that obvious, it is easy to see how the error took hold and got out of line, especially when extrabiblical texts are studied more than scripture itself.

A Practical Exercise Visualizes Five-Fold Significance

Scripture places the pastor fourth in God's line of New Creation church ministers, and not third (and certainly not first). Nonetheless, an entire multi-century institution was built upon the error; apostles and prophets are passé and the pastors occupy their stead with bishops replacing apostles in church headship. Further contradicting this glaring error is Paul's contrasting list of 1 Corinthians 12:28, 29 where apostles and prophets are also listed first. That the Lord by His Spirit moved Paul to list the apostle and prophet as God's first officers three times in the two letters is significant and a sure indication that His apostle to the Gentiles meant what he wrote and was convinced it came from the Lord Himself. As with any text, Paul's order of words is important. It is no different with his listing of the apostle and the prophet. When one thinks of how the Lord uses His ministers and their foundations, structure, functions and operations, God's rationale becomes obvious. Listing the first three officers in Ephesians 4:11 as apostle, prophet, and evangelist is, or should be considered, significant. For God it was evidently deliberate, especially when 1

6

Corinthians 12:28, 29 say nothing about the *evangelist* or the *pastor*, which should also be seen as noteworthy.

One reason Paul chose this order is that the apostle and prophet are foundational officers. Their calling begins with a message received directly from the Lord's mouth that succeeds in attracting the following that transforms into a church. The first two officers in Ephesians 4:11 are distinct from the pastor and teacher mainly because their work begins outside and usually starts without a following. These two officers take the risen Christ to the world and convert its penitents to the church.

The pastor's work however, begins entirely different. For instance, pastors' ministries do not start until apostles and evangelists have been successful. Once the followings they gather enter the church, the pastor's mantle is activated. Upon this sequence of events rests the pastor's ministry. Taking away the pastor's congregation alleviates the premise of his or her ministry. This being true, the pastor's chief role then is to house and host those brought into the Lord's kingdom in local assemblies that are also called congregations. Here is one of the many primary reasons why the pastor has much to risk in returning the church to God's divine order. Aside from upsetting the sheep, there are numerous concerns over the pastor's interaction with apostles and prophets as ordained by the Lord. Pastors are understandably troubled about their place and stability in a work most of them have devoted their lives to building. They wonder if this divine order, or better yet for our purposes, biblical order, is a better term, meaning the pastor looses his or her flock and livelihood. Will apostles assume control over congregations worldwide and if so how does that live out in the congregations? Overall, the question that begs answering is what is the apostle and prophet's role today?

Building a church is hard and takes years of hard work with long days and constant trials, tribulations, and upheavals. The last thing anyone wants is that those who have done so be rewarded with evil for the years of good that they have done. Anyone with God's mind knows that is not His way. There remains before us the task of conforming to scripture or abandoning it altogether in favor of popular trends and carnal whims. Pastors may preside over their congregations but they are not by virtue of doing so its ultimate head, in God's mind, if for no other reason than they generally inherit their members and do not necessarily, often infrequently, births them into the kingdom.

The teacher too relies on a following for his or her office, only this following is not called a flock or sheep, but a class of students. In order for the teacher to educate their following, their students or learners must come to them, or have gathered somewhere in some

7

kind of classroom setting. Even today's distance learning trend cannot limit this reality. At some point, the student and teacher will have to come face to face, even if only electronically. For the teacher to know the success of his or her efforts, they must somehow analyze the effects of their labors. This is usually by testing their learners to confirm their knowledge was accurately received and understood. Conscientious teachers routinely want to do this by meeting their learners at least once or twice during the learning teaching process. Like the pastor, the teacher's mantle is activated once a learner has attached to them. Until then the teacher like the pastor has nothing to do. With apostles and prophets, it is radically different. Their work begins once the Lord speaks to them. These mantles are activated by divine initiative and not prior minister results; that is apostles and prophets ministries are not dependent upon earthly ignition but upon heavenly initiatives. In these contexts, commission triggers the work and not merely a calling.

Apostles, prophets, and evangelists are the church's primary itinerant ministers. They take their messages from God and declare to the world and as a result gather and deposit the members of Christ's body to its stationary laborers, pastors, and teachers. Therefore, Paul's repetitive order makes perfect sense to God and when corrected, His church will see its wisdom as well.

A Summary of How Each Officer Sees the World, Church, and Ministry

The following material gives just a brief overview of the most prominent expressions of the Ephesians 4:11 officers to show how and why the Church should actively seek to conform to the Lord's divine order. It is by no means exhaustive but is included to prepare you for the exhaustive individual treatment of each officer presented in the next book in this series. Beginning with the third officer in the lineup, this section closes its discussion on the apostle and prophet.

The Evangelist

Evangelists see the world as a giant mission field where people must be saved to escape its doom and destruction, as they should. They are concerned with rescuing as many souls from death and eternal damnation as possible. Not inherently wrong within itself, the problem arises in the means and method they are assigned to accomplish their ends. This mantle concentrates on wooing and winning souls from the world to God. Discussions of judgment that frighten or chase people away only enter the evangelist's message when souls are wavering on repentance, conversion, and God's judgment on those that reject Him. Evangelists as heralds of the good

8

news center on God's love, grace, mercy, and forgiveness. Theirs is, of necessity, a matter of numbers because evangelists can only measure their fruit by their numbers. They ordinarily cannot linger in a life long enough to nurture a convert to full Christian maturity. Leading souls to Jesus, as it is called, requires the evangelist to conduct what is traditionally recognized as an altar call. Those who repeat the salvation prayer and acknowledge Jesus as their Personal Savior are taken at their word to have been saved. Once this is achieved, the evangelist, unless he or she has a church, moves on to the next audience or penitent to repeat the cycle. Rarely does this officer spend sufficient time to instruct and settle a new convert into Christ's body. That is usually the work of the pastorate or a teacher.

The sheer nature of the office's execution resolves that the ministry of the evangelist be mainly a numbers game. Getting the new Christian mature and productive in Christ comes under apostleship, the pastor, or teacher; even the prophet can take up some of this duty if this mantle's revelatory, teaching side is emphasized. Because evangelists' chief role is winning souls to Jesus Christ, they are not relied upon to produce, if you will, a quality Christian. For evangelists, this is typically not feasible if the mantle is executed correctly. Their call to the itinerate prohibits them from spending that kind of time with their new converts. Routinely they must return to the work of replenishing God's body with new believers. No better scripture example exists to confirm this truth than the ministry of Philip the evangelist. His was an itinerant circuit where he traveled from city to city, preaching Jesus Christ. Even though powerful signs and wonders attended Philip's ministry, his call was never to settle in one place for too long. The incident with the Ethiopian Eunuch underscores this truth. Philip preached the scriptures to the man, explained Jesus Christ, and baptized the eunuch into Christ's body. As if to make the point that the evangelist is to keep moving and converting, while the eunuch was rejoicing in his conversion the Holy Spirit whisks Philip off to his next assignment to preach and convert others to Jesus Christ (see Acts 8:12-17, 39, 40). By this means, evangelists rapidly spread and increase His Church. Perhaps because today's churches have been dominated by the spirit of the evangelist, they are so numbers conscious, equating volume and quantity to quality.

The Pastor

The pastor's mantle is not much different from the evangelists, in that it too finds its validity in the lives of people. Pastors see their mantle's primary obligation as placing people in the church more than establishing them in God's kingdom dominions. If the evangelist is concerned with the field of the world and finds it difficult to relate to

9

the ecclesia's domestic matters, the pastor's views are confined to domesticity, making them unable to relate to fieldwork or the immediacy of the kingdom's eternality. Pastors' mantles find their validity in the lives of people by focusing mainly on the local church. They are concerned that it remains staffed and occupied with sound Christians. The pastors' mantles perform their chief obligation by housing people in the church. Once they become members, pastors' focus expands to concentrate on positively hosting their congregations to keep them in God's household—again not wrong, just limited. Of necessity, this too can become principally a numbers venture as the more members the more validation a pastor believes he or she gets. Many pastors do a wonderful job of nurturing their people but the fact remains that without a congregation, a pastor is disemployed and merely a minister. As the ecclesia's primary domestic, the pastor typifies the proverbial homemaker. He or she sees the world narrowly through the eyes of the household, which is how the pastor's mantle is confirmed. They are not going to risk emptying their churches by loosing sheep to controversial messages such as those likely to come from apostles and prophets. These mantles benefit the mature Christian most of all, something the writer of Hebrews 5:9-6:3 realized.

The Teacher

For the teacher the principle holds that no students equal no ministry. It is just that simple. If the ecclesia's domestic, primary caregiver and nurturer is the pastor, the teacher would be then classed as its secondary one, seeing the new convert essentially in academic terms. Though care giving is not their principal focus, edification is and so teachers are validated when they have pupils. Teachers being unavoidably analytical are very often critical and diagnostic in their views of the new convert; an often unsettling attitude is integral to the nature of the office. Teachers are designed to recognize and dislike ignorance for they know it to be the source of destruction, disadvantage, and impoverishment. Their keen instincts are ever on the lookout for information and knowledge deficits that can rob a young or uneducated convert of the full benefits of the Lord's covenant. A true teacher despises that possibility and so can appear relentless in his or her call to remove ignorance. They are vigilant in their aim to prevent or minimize error and the consequences that come with it.

What all these offices share is a distribution of God's revealed word as received by His apostles and prophets firsthand. These two offices (apostle and prophet) are intended to dispense active revelations from God that once received, pass onto the remaining three offices to inculcate throughout the body. Each of the remaining

10

three members dispenses his or her portion of apostolic and prophetic revelations according to the ministry emphases of his or her mantle. The evangelist uses it to persuade a soul to convert to Jesus Christ, the pastor to motivate church membership and attendance, and the teacher to disciple and settle the saints to the Lord's culture. What they all lack is the immediate audience with the Lord that dispenses such information.

Apostles & Prophets

Apostles and prophets receive revelations and insights from the Lord directly similar to that which His Old Testament prophets and all the New Testament apostles received to deliver their fresh manna to the world. Apostles and prophets are inducted into the Lord's firsthand by and absorbed into what has become the Creator's holy word and His eternal world. They experience God's kingdom citizens and receive revelations directly and dramatically as His first ranking agents. John's Apocalypse and the record of Zechariah 3 demonstrating Joshua the high priest's induction both make this statement.

In addition, apostles and prophets, because of their extensive interaction with the Risen Lord, see the new convert and indeed the Church at large in radically different terms than the other officers. Both agents recognize the ecclesia's call to mirror the Lord's eternal kingdom. Their approach to ministry pursues a reflection of the everlasting kingdom of God and Christ, in the same way that the moon reflects the light of the sun to shine in the darkness. Another way of expressing this truth, aside from the use of the word *embassy* mentioned elsewhere in this text is to say that that the ecclesia's on earth is ordained to serve the Lord as a massive *satellite* of His eternal world. It is created to work in tandem with His spiritual world and its institutions as tributaries mirroring the activities of the unseen. That is why and how the church and the planet are perpetually cared for, and indisputably governed by the Almighty's celestial beings. It explains as well why both are inseparably tied to their existence and influence. It is also how those born to darkness, sin, and death can gain insight into the Creator's everlasting orders.

Apostles and prophets seek to illuminate the otherwise hidden aspects, agencies and powers of eternity's sovereignty and dispense their logic in a way that vivifies the heavenly schema that portrays immortality to mortals. The ecclesia's chief purpose, beyond this is to illuminate the darkened, human mind with its Creator's wisdom and ideally reconnect the unsaved to their eternal creaturehood as children of light rather than offspring of the supernatural darkness they pursue. Their call is to sanctify for Him the body He prepared for His eternity existence by partnering with His Christlike dominion. Apostles and

11

prophets start out grasping fully the Lord's reasons for propelling His Church toward its everlasting destiny. They instinctually comprehend its vast purpose as eternity's long awaited cohabitant. Apostles however, outpace the others in this objective by acting as Christ's catalytic agents; increasingly unfolding the mysteries of God's hidden worlds to those born into Christ's body. They alone are ascribed the privilege and duty in scripture as <u>stewards</u> of God's mysteries, see 1 Corinthians 4:1,2. Apostles are privy to the secret and silent workings of the Lord's invisible world and are given aspects of it to dispense to the body of Christ in their seasons.

Apostles and prophets keenly and skillfully deliver to God's Church the single power that is able to save their souls and challenge them to transform into Christ's image and likeness. That is God's unadulterated word. Apostles bring the Lord's truth home to the Christian's heart and soul, incisively influencing every area of life, directly or not, to motivate living Christ's life every day. Vague disconnected preaching and teaching will generally not come from these two officers. They know all too well how severe and glorious the Lord is. The nature of the apostles' and prophets' induction to the Godhead's service make them privy to His kingdom, tasting it sometimes personally in order to persuade people by God's word of truth put into their mouths. They learn from their divine intimacy not only that heaven and hell are real but also how God's holiness prevents Him from giving eternal life to those that reject or pervert His way of life.

At times, this seems brutal, and as said earlier only the mature saint of God can withstand it: the Christian that has suffered with God, felt His hot displeasure and stinging correction. Such saints have faced squarely God's sovereignty without the traditional coddling, divine revelation, or superficial explanations the other officers rely on to persuade believers of His love. Apostles and prophets know what it means to say that God's will be done and how He expects His body to surrender to that will. They also understand His Church's duty toward His sovereignty; that is to trust and obey. Aaron's loss of his two presumptuous sons in Leviticus 10:1-3 exemplifies this. Apostles and prophets are furthermore groomed to recognize the limits of salvation's liberty the Lord allows and informs His people of the recklessness of presumption and arrogance. Their messages are not often couched in terms that console the flesh, but occasionally they seem to deliberately select phrases and vernacular that cannot help but inflame it. Bluntness and sometimes, frontal honesty permeate these ministers' messages as piercing insight joins discomforting relevance to set captive souls free or raise their defenses to release the hidden rebellion that moves them to flee to safer sermons. God is truth and His apostles and prophets are bound by a peculiar dispensational

12

restraint to utter that truth even when it is evident that it will be ignored or attacked. Lastly, these two offices are how the Church gets its fresh streams of wisdom and share of unfolding mysteries and revelations for their generations. Apostles and prophets receive doctrine and distill it for the body to add to its present and prior theology and move on to the next level of Christian development that can only come from new revelations.

Another Problem with Modern Five-Fold Views

If the only problem with the church's handling of God's E-4 offices were altering the list, our work here would be finished. However, it is not because there is much more to address. The misapplication tactic did not end with merely misquoting the scripture's text. It went dangerously further. With apostles multiplying and manifesting at a rapid rate, it behooves apostles and prophets to step up and avert a repeat of the mistake that brought us to this place in the first place. The last time the church seriously took up this subject, its first two officers were excised from its ministry ranks altogether, a bold step that birthed the erroneous misquoting just discussed. It allowed the void to be filled with just three of the five ministers.

To demonstrate how ludicrous the whole concept is, when I teach about the five-fold, I have my learners attempt to pick up their pens or pencils with just the last three fingers and try to sign their names. When they attempt to do so, they witness firsthand how awkward it is to do. While many of them can get it done, they all conclude that what ends up on their papers is not their legal or legitimate signature. Part two of the exercise requires them to put the writing instrument down and pick it up again, this time with the last three fingers locked in their palms and the forefinger (pointer) and the thumb finger gripping their pen or pencil. Here is where the activity gets interesting as they do so with relative ease. They find that they can better write their names with these two than anything else.

The signature used this time to write is more like their own with the stress associated with using the pointer and thumb to sign it less than it was when they used the claw. However, to complete the lesson, the learners are asked their conclusion. Invariably, it is that even though they can write their names better with the first two fingers of their hand, they cannot handle anything else with as much ease and miss the bracing support the remaining three fingers give any writer. The lesson is learned: While the church has been able to get much done dividing the digits of God's hand to suit popular theology, God has accomplished little as a result. Try the exercise yourself and you will see the obstacles God faces, since the five-fold ministry is referred to in scripture as the hand of God. The class continues.

Five-Fold or...

From here we turn our attention to the conflict over the use of the term five-fold for the hand versus the popular "ascension gifts." Here again a simple comparison is used to resolve the conflict. Students are asked if the names of the church's ministry offices existed prior to the Lord's coming and how He injected them into the world. The five-fold/hand issue hinges on whether or not the Lord Jesus' ascension birthed into the world the titles that did not previously exist. That is, did the titles of apostle, prophet, evangelist, pastor, teacher exist among God's people prior to His incarnation and ascension? I submit that all but two of them did if we base it upon the prophecy of Psalm 68:18. With the exception of the apostle and the evangelist, all the titles existed before Christ's incarnation and ascension; the prophet, the pastor, and the teacher were standing institutions in Israel.

In the church's constitutional text of 1 Corinthians 12:28, 29, the prophet and teacher are brought forward as ordinal ministries of the New Creation church. There are good grounds for accepting Moses as an Old Testament apostle under what the early Jews named the *shaliach*. Being sent by God to Pharaoh to bring His people out of bondage meets the "sent one" definition of the apostle as well as His atypical induction into Yahweh's service. His unusual interactions with the Lord are recorded in Numbers 12:7, 8 and Deuteronomy 34:10-14. His characteristic apostleship ministry is especially evident in the extraordinary miracles, signs, and wonders the man performed to decimate the entire kingdom of Egypt, a then formidable world power.

The pastor, as an express term existed and used by Jeremiah and Ezekiel, was called a shepherd. Isaiah exemplifies the Old Testament evangelist, even though he was a prophet, since his prophecies preached the redemptive work of the Lord Jesus being granted to the whole world. Moreover, the entire Ephesians 4:11 staff is concealed in the writings of the prophets and the apostles and based on scripture. Christ's high priestly work is secreted in His earthly reinstitution as Melchizedek's eternal priesthood sequestered in Genesis' archetypal Salem (Jerusalem) from the line of Judah. Thus, we see how the five-fold always functioned in the Bible. They were merely, like the remainder of the Lord's Old Testament kingdom, departments, and officiations carried over to the church. Ephesians 4:11 frankly fulfills Psalm 68:18: *"Thou hast ascended on high, thou hast led captivity captive: thou hast **received** gifts for men; yea, **for the rebellious also**, that the LORD God might dwell among them."* Those gifts were given to the rebellious that are now rendered obedient by the new birth. Now they show up with two new additions, the apostle, and the evangelist.

In any event, to return to the discussion of the appropriateness of the term five fold, I point the students to Hosea 12:10, the one time the word *ministry* is used in the Old Testament. Minister, however, is there sixty-six times. In the plural ministries appears twice and ministering shows up two times as well. The word *ministry* however is there once, applied to the *ministry of the prophets*. The word scripture translators settled on to express it in relation to their ministries is *yad*, the Hebrew word for *hand*. Its meanings spans from the open hand to the hand as used in oaths, vows, services, and work for handling details and tasks. Ancient hand metaphor appears to be the premise the Lord Jesus draws from in His ministry as Moses' Great Prophet.

Two Mantles that Did Not Contribute to the New Testament

To further answer five-fold validity and the strongholds hindering its proper order in the church's leadership spectrum, one has to return to the only authority the true Christian church has, that of God's holy word. The scriptures are the only place to find the New Creation ecclesia, its eternal kanon, and its leadership guidelines. In order to assure one arrives at the Lord's conclusion on His scriptures, in particular the Ephesians 4:11 offices along with 1 Corinthians 12:28, 29, one has to accept that, as stated before, the apostle's mantle is the only one that penned the New Testament. That means the apostles instituted church government and canonized scripture for the church. The implications of that revelation and its affects ripple throughout the church world, and they are staggering.

Considering what is distilled today as church doctrine was manufactured without God's apostles and the prophets, whose wisdom upon which rests the church's foundation, indeed the whole of Judeo-Christian theology, we must wonder how accurate its ministry doctrine really is. If the church's two founding mantles had little or no part in modern Christian theology's development, how reliable is today's evangelical pastoral treatment of the subject. For instance, in regards to the latter that the two officers responsible for receiving God's revelation of church doctrine have been ignored in the culling of ministry counsel and organizational principles is disturbing. Furthermore, that the two mantles not mentioned in the church's ministry constitution nor recognized by the early apostles as contributors to classic church order and structure may not be the best choice for defining the Ephesians 4:11 staff. Eternal kingdom credibility and the divine wisdom for purposefully allocating each one's place and function in Christ's church may be lacking. As uncomfortable as it may be to resolve, the New Testament has no pastors or evangelists contributing to its writings, especially the

15

epistles that are written entirely by apostles. That Timothy and Titus, two epistles that deal with the church and shepherding, may be dubbed pastoral books is a stretch, since the author giving the counsel and imparting the wisdom is the apostle Paul. Otherwise, no epistle writings are attributed to pastors or evangelists, but only to apostles.

If the mantles of the pastor and evangelist, nor the teacher for that matter, never received the revelation of the church or its structure, how are they able to define and govern it today on their own? Given that mantles do not leave the planet but merely devolve to the next generations it would seem that by divine design, they are incapable of doing so. For instance, Joshua inherited Moses' mantle, Elisha received Elijah's, John the Baptist received Elijah's, and Jesus was mistaken for a resurrected Old Testament prophet (Mark 6:16; 8:27, 28). Perhaps that is why the church today is out of divine order and struggling with fundamental regard for God, His order, and His government. When I looked at the *Ministries Today* article, these factors struck me as odd. Having gone to their website to see the pastors' discussion board on apostles and prophets (I saw no prophetic or apostolic representation), I wondered what other institution on earth would do such a thing. I wondered what professional organization would take it upon itself to define order and govern another that they have no comparable insight, experience, education, or aptitudes to substantiate their opinions. As a case in point, an electrician would not define and institute regulations for a doctor, lawyer, judge, or police officer if he or she had no knowledge or experience in the field. Yet we have the fourth in the line of Ephesians 4:11 ministers taking it upon themselves to do just that for God's apostles and prophets, the first two in the divine lineage of New Creation church ministers.

If history is not to repeat itself and to avoid landing in this place again as a church, it behooves today's apostles and prophets to step up and define themselves clearly for their times and the future. While it is wonderful to gather with one's peers and colleagues to discuss the technical aspects and the professional protocols of the mantles, the real test is how what is discussed and resolved is communicated and mainstreamed to the masses. As it stands today, the only ones who enjoy discovering and understanding apostleship and the prophetic are those called to the office. The people conditioned by evangelism or theologically predisposed to the mantles of the pastor and the teacher are terrified. They feel threatened, confused, and at risk for potential abuse. These factors helped previous leaders assure their positions, and their teachings and beliefs are all the church knows.

CHAPTER TWO

On the Subject of Titles

Chapter Topics

The Importance of Titles • What Is A Title? • Defining a Title •
About Authority • What is a Title? • Titles Back in Time • Founding
an Institution • Officers Staff Institutions • Titles Began Divine •
Traditional Church View of Titles • Titles Do Not Infect Hearts—
Infected Hearts Corrupt Titles & Positions • What Comes From
Within Defiles • Suggested Assignment

Did Jesus bring the titles "apostle" and "evangelist" to earth as part of His ongoing redemptive campaign and are they related to the message He was sent to preach? The question leads one to wonder if He brought the two titles from eternity or if He coined them from secular or pagan vocabularies expressly for His own ministry purposes. If neither of these is the case, then we would have to conclude that the two terms not directly seen in the Old Testament's classes of ministries, the *apostle* and *evangelist*, were in operation somewhere during Jesus' earthly ministry. If in all likelihood they were, under what circumstances were they used and how did they become common language used by His scribes to record His ministry?

Though we have addressed misquoting, misapplication, misalignment, and the validity of the hand symbolism for identifying

17

the Ephesians 4:11 ministers, two barriers seriously impede the church's pursuit of scripture's divine order. They are a misunderstanding of the roles, titles, offices, functions and giftings found in God's structure and the fact that anything we have today remotely addressing the subject on a wide scale is either pastoral or evangelical, or a blend of both.

The Importance of Titles

Now to discuss the last bastion against God's restoration of apostolic and prophetic authority over His church: that is the subject of titles. Titles are names organizations and institutions give to those authorized by their founders or authorities to act in its stead and by the power of its name. A gift driven church mentality, although it conforms to this truth everyday, fails to grasp the overriding importance of assigning titles to those who would represent it and its God in any official capacity. Official in this context refers to acting in His name with the expectation of yielding a particular result (outcome) or end product. Any actions generally intended by their performers to be taken seriously fit this description. However, apart from the covering of some lawful and recognized institution endorsing or upholding a person's words and deeds in the name or stead of an authority, those exercising their *gift* are mere freelancers in the kingdom. They have no authorized right or delegated authority, or even a legitimate outlet to carry out any official function in the name of the Lord. Titles more than capacitate, they legitimize a talent, or gifting's right to pursue a specified goal or carry out a particular function. This reality is subscribed to everyday as people go to jobs and wear name badges that designate their rank, level, and admittance limitations in their companies. Daily, as a modern society citizens meet and comply with workers backed by titles for the sake of the institutions they represent, the order they imperceptibly impose and the expertise and wisdom their titles imply. The subtle tactic that downplayed the authority of pastors and set them up for sheep abuse, rejection, and resistance is being repeated with God's restoration of apostles and prophets. It is all based upon the legitimate right of a minister of the Lord Jesus Christ to use titles. For the most part, apostles and prophets are being castigated, a first line of defense, for desiring, to use titles to fortify their reinstatement and right to head church leadership. Their decision greatly conflicts with the popular trend that took hold several decades ago.

Classic Definitions of a Minister

A minister was viewed quite differently during the Bible's formative eras than today. Seeing every entity birthed by a divine being as the injection of a new kingdom and thus government in the earth, those that represented their progenitor deities were seen as agents of both worlds. On the one hand, the minister served his or her deity as an agent of the other world. On the hand, the minister functioned as an official intermediary between the two worlds assuring the citizens of the god's territory learned, understood, and obeyed their celestial monarch. Below are some of the terms that were applied to this responsibility. After reading them, observe how well they establish the work, duties, scope, and influence a minister hand before secularism ruled.

The Title *Minister* Encompasses the Following Synonyms

1. Dean	2. Agent	3. Aide
4. Ambassador	5. Envoy	6. Diplomat
7. Executive	8. Official	9. Plenipotentiary
10. Premier	11. Prime Minister	12. Chief of State
13. Governmental Head	14. Chancellor	15. Administrator
16. Steward	17. Governor	18. Judge
19. Leader	20. Overseer	21. President
22. Negotiator	23. Operator	24. Operative
25. Subsidy		

Twenty-five terms express, what a minister was understood as in earlier eras. Those listed above shed light on the basis of the authority inherent in the offices people enter upon being installed in God's service.

Today's ministers feeling themselves more sophisticated than their predecessors have agreed as a collective guild of professionals to forego the use of titles, both with each other and with their beneficiaries. The tactic, quite effective to date, silently (maybe informally) decrees that church leaders, with the possible exception of the pastor depending on the religious camp, were not inclined nor worthy of titular regard. The long-term fallout from this action is that Christian clergy need not be accorded or seen as deserving the respect such titles award other professional fields. Contending that the Lord does not and never intended for one position to exercise authority over another irrespective of Paul's deliberate use of them in Ephesians 4:11 and 1 Corinthians 12:28, 29, modern ministers subtly erased the boundaries that distinguished the minister from the body. Consequently, they stripped the use of titles from all ministry positions and leveled them for the sake of minister and congregational equality. Here are two scenarios to underscore the point.

Imagine walking into a church with people gathered or mulling about and being introduced to everyone in the room by your first name. Now think about what changes when you step up to the front to gain the attention of the others in order to be heard and regarded. Unless people have a reason to interrupt their conversations and listen, the speaker is likely to be ignored, ridiculed, or rejected. The best way to be accepted and heard by an unfamiliar group is by giving a title if the purpose of being in their midst is to publicly address them. To simply say, "I am so and so" to a group of people and begin addressing them when they have no idea why they should listen to a speaker is futile. People respond to authority by way of titles, and without one being announced, public talks can be disregarded. A distracted audience consumed with questions about who is speaking, why they should listen, and what is the point of what is being said can frustrate a speech.

It appears Christian leaders love the idea of blending in with their masses in every possible way, not a problem in itself. Eager to show their elevation to service in God's ministry is no big deal, they go to extremes to remain one of the *gang*, so to speak. Truly, humility is certainly godly and the Lord does not expect us to laud one position over the other, but it takes more than a title to constitute abuse or to make people to feel abused by one in authority. Blending ranks with the masses often has the affect of frustrating a leader's accountability to God and diminishing their influence with the people. Consequently, the "title-less minister" tactic backfires and almost appears deceptive. Surely, it is disarming. A minister's friendship with the flock and concern for its comfort should not be allowed to dilute the official authority the Lord needs His leaders to exercise in His name. Those to benefit from a leader's position should feel at ease with them but not to the point of anticipating leniency as a result. Quality steps should be taken to assure that ease does not the breed familiarity that fosters and/or promotes casualness and disrespect.

People have to know who their leaders are and what they may expect from them. They need to recognized and resolve why their leaders should be trusted. The best way to do this is a practice that goes way back in time. It has been done historically by assigning various actions, functions, authorities, and titles. That is how people immediately recognize their direct and indirect authority figures. Titles have the effect of quickly allaying fears regarding who is backing those in authority and in a word say who and what the leader is to an organization, group or department. Followers need to, deserve to, understand the nature and extent of what backs their leaders. They crave to recognize how worthwhile trusting and obeying a Christian is to their standing with the Lord. Many of them seriously want to know how their leadership interactions comply with His eternal destiny for their lives. Traditionally and legally it is required that senders, superiors, and sovereigns formally authorize entitled officers to act on their behalf. Some certified notification should sufficiently inform and

20

educate those dispatched on the nature and scope of their positions. In addition, senders ought to include in their dispatch *commission* letters that inform those to whom their official is sent of who the officer is and what he or she is sent to perform. Here is where being *called* is frankly separated from being *dispatched* or delegated.

In a formal communication, senders describe the terms, conditions, and extent of their dispatched representatives' assignments. Authentic communications detail the level of power and authority sent ones have been granted by their sending authorities. Well-scripted senders' communiqués have the effect of naming (entitling) their dispatched officers and stating their sphere of authority. This is to motivate obedience, conversion, cooperation, alliance, or allegiance to the sender on the recipient's part.

Such communications are normally sent to authority figures in distant locations where the official is sent to serve as their senders' extensions to accomplish what the sender would if he or she were present. Officer integrity dictates that sent ones immediately and constantly put those they serve in mind of their senders, the true authorities in their land. The officer is to, so closely model their conduct, behavior, attitudes, perspectives, and conversation after their senders that it is virtually impossible for the duration of the assignment to detect any functional difference between the sender and, his or her official representative.

All these fine points should be in the official communications so that it conforms to established ambassadorial protocol. The sender's language should alert receiving authorities of a new authority figure's arrival in their land, announcing and explaining the reasons they were dispatched to them. The receiving authority should also be told how the sender expects or hopes his or her delegate be received, treated and trusted by those to ultimately establish their sent one's place, purpose, and business in their territories. Worded effectively, the communication enables distant authorities to consent to authorize visitors' actions in their territories.

From the angel in Moses' burning bush to Jesus' appearance, after John the Baptist's announcement, this practice has been commonplace in all societies. For modern societies, it is no different. Strangers must be announced and powerful strangers must notify the powers in distant territories of any agents they send (dispatch or commission) to them. Companies, clubs and organizations, courts, militaries, and civil agencies all practice this and we live with it daily. Yet when it comes to the church, somehow the rules and protocols relax in favor of vague ambivalent spirituality. However, God being orderly and lawful--He for the sake of legitimacy follows the protocol He set to avoid His spiritual and natural authorities rejection of His dispatched or commissioned agents. To convey His mind, will and desires, He sent messages, used the established message systems and postal carriers. The Lord identified and classified His own couriers and empowered them with incomparable signature signs, wonders, and miracles to persuade those they met that indeed He had sent them. The Lord backed their words and impressed upon whosoever He willed to perform them in the earth.

Today, the pattern still holds as the Lord Jesus Christ continues to summon, inform, empower, commission and authorize His representatives in every generation to continue His work. He entitles them as ordained by God before the foundation of the world, and dispatches them to the churches under the Holy Spirit's escort. By the Spirit He announces and confirms who each minister is to Him and to His church. The Holy Spirit plainly declares on many occasions and in many ways what God's officers are, what class of minister they occupy, and broadly describes what they are sent by God to minister to His body. Today's divinely authorized agents, then, should publicize their identity to those affected by their ministries to inspire the trust that motivates obedience and cooperation.

People need to know who and what is being sent to them in the name of the Lord and the extent of power given to their leaders. They should clearly grasp the distinct role each member of the Ephesians 4:11 staff fills and recognize each one's mantle in action. Additionally, God's people should well understand authority in general and how the Lord expects them to submit to His, as Hebrews 13:17 exhorts. The Christian church should realize that the New Testament does not negate authority but only prescribes parameters for its exercise. Paul said that it was for edification and not destruction.

All this should be made clear to those the Lord admonishes His church to heed. Here is what God and man's induction and dispatch of authority figures to territorial leaders is really all about; the titles say what it means to be appointed, anointed, and installed into an office by the Lord. If sending and empowering superiors or sovereigns do not identify the place(s) or position(s) they create for their officials to achieve their purposes, those to benefit from their delegated authorities' actions and initiatives will reject their officials. Confusion backlash may well lead them to despise their authority, disregard and seek to overthrow their leaders' positions. That is what the Lord did through the apostle Paul and others in His holy word. It communicates continually who His authority figures are and how they are authorized by His Holy Spirit in the planet. Because Jesus is forever alive and the Holy Spirit cannot die, there is neither reason nor provision for changing God's original program.

The Spirit of the Lord is still working out His redemptive program in the world, and God's word— Christ, the Logos—is still living and powerful. That is the beauty of how God set it all up and how He assures His perfect plan remains unchanged. Having its origins and roots in eternity where the principal operations are makes it as eternal and everlasting as the God that ordained and imposed it on flesh. That is also how the Lord shut mortal humanity out of its alterations forever. Christ "ever liveth" says Hebrews 7:25; because His is an unchangeable priesthood, He cannot die. Moreover, since God granted Him the power of an endless life, neither He nor the angels of the seven churches need replacement, improvement, or a new plan—all the reasons revisions are necessary in the first place. Jesus, the apostle John witnesses, is the eternal, immortal, invisible God-King; and according to 1 Timothy 1:17: *"Now unto the King eternal, immortal, invisible, the only wise God, be honour and glory for ever and ever. Amen."* These words to the carnal mind mean little, but to the eternal mind renewed by God's Spirit, they say much.

If something is eternal and immortal then anything pertaining to death is powerless against it. If it is invisible then all the machinations of the visible world are futile and cannot undo it. Attempting to do so is about as senseless as trying to attack and destroy the wind, the sky, or electricity. One may be able to harness and manipulate them to a point, but doing away with them altogether is impossible.

The Bible does not stand just because people love it; it remains because people become it. Initially met on paper written with pen and ink, the Holy Spirit sees that Christ's people conform to scripture because He transfers what is printed to the human heart, mind, will, and soul. As long as God's Spirit remains in the earth, His pervasive global influence will reach and continue to embed the human soul (psyche) with the mind and sentiments of the living God and the Risen Christ. Jesus got it right the first time and was rewarded with eternal everything. His triumph made it safe for the Lord to close out His word with what we have today, confident that there are sufficient patterns for us to follow throughout all time.

What is a Title?

Titles, the name of jobs, offices, and positions, in addition to what has been said, empower the range and limits of authority that may be exercised by one installed or employed in a given position. They permit people who enter an office to exercise some type of authority and are as important to positions as the first and last names given to individuals. Names identify family line and persona and many surnames are lineal, genealogical, and/or geographical, carrying great influence within their societies. Similarly, titles are equally important as the names of professions. They help us recognize and respect societal, governmental, religious, or civil officials and cooperate with them. Titles divulge in single terms or phrases the diverse business contained within them.

Here is another introductory scenario relating the importance of titles. You have a relative in the hospital in need of prayer. You call your minister asking for a special visit for your loved one who is in the hospital seriously ill. Your minister agrees and immediately leaves for the hospital; you believe time is short. Upon entering the lobby, the minister is asked his or her name and business. Your minister responds with a first name only, foregoing the title for humility sake. The clerk at the desk or the security person asks your casually dressed minister if he or she is a member of the family (usually the immediate family is meant). Your minister replies, "No." The clerk continues, "What is the nature of your relationship with the patient?" Your minister says, "I am the pastor." The clerk's attitude changes because the title makes your minister's visit clear. Adding the title short-circuited all necessary explanations by giving your minister, the credibility needed, for the desk clerk to authorize that all important visit to your critically ill relative. Had your minister initially said, "I am a pastor," the process would have been quicker.

It would have mattered little if you previously put your pastor on the visitor's list as Pastor so-and-so, if he or she still simply said "I am so-and-so and I am here to visit," unless you listed your pastor by his or her first name. Putting the minister on the visitor list certainly would have gotten them in to see the patient, but make no mistake about it, you did not, despite your first name relationship with your minister, expect the visit to be merely casual or comforting. You called your minister to visit your loved one because of his or her divinely official capacity. You expect something to come out of that visit that no other visitor could deliver, and that is the point of this discussion.

Titles alone stand on their own; mere first names do not. It gained your pastor entry into the patient's room, and once he or she entered, you expected the release of God's power to intercede with the disease. Your call to your minister indicates you believe the minister holds some standing in the supernatural that authorizes him or her to overpower the natural world. That position, enabled by a title and office, you believe can heal your loved one or prepare them for the afterlife. Inwardly, you know that when a minister prays it travels a different circuit and gains more direct access to God. If that is true, why pretend that it is not so by downplaying the titles that identify the ministers' status and influence as the Lord's divine officer? Why minimize God's servants and their ecclesiastical offices by refusing to acknowledge them and yet still expect their results? John the Baptist encountered a similar situation in

John 1:19-27 when people thought he was the Messiah. Understanding his call to pave the way for the Messiah, John distinguished his duty and title from that of the coming Messiah.

Defining a Title

A title names a professional or vocational position or job into which a person enters by installation, appointment, or employment. Titles are important because they identify in a single term or phrase the scope of work, duties, responsibilities, station, and authority of a particular line of work. Titles, assigned once job, duty, or responsibility descriptions have been defined, give an organization levels, positions, and service classifications for its workers (or servants). Titles rely on delegated assignments. To be legitimate, they must relate to *functions* that identify their scope and limits, and explain the nature of their activities or operations as delegated by the position's duly authorized higher officials.

To be received by those for whom a function or assignment was officially created, or to whom a functionary (an official) is sent, the position with its benefits, powers, and authority must be named for recognition, cooperation, and respect. In other words, something must tell the empowered officer the intents of his or her post and its affect on the overall organizational scheme. Officers should know what gives them the legitimate right to perform or serve in that capacity. The legitimate right to accomplish this is dispensed in the license to occupy and execute the office. Hiring papers, work assignments, or authorized commission delegacies commute the principal's powers to his or her appointee. It allows a stranger's intervention in another's affairs as a delegate. Official delegation comes from the position's authorizing agency or principal, the one to whom the entire original task was given in the first place. Presumably, according to Ecclesiastes 5:8, NKJV, the original delegacy was received from a higher official, a legal, national, or divine sovereign entity. Here is how it works.

The initial delegatory power *breaks off* portions of his or her vast task and assigns them to offices created and empowered for others to act in their name or in their stead just as they would if they themselves were executing the office. In doing so, the delegator shares with lower offices incremental measures of the duties, labors, powers, authority and responsibility correspondent with the subordinate positions complexity, intent, and station. This allows concentrated portions of the segmented tasks to be handled separately with the degree of attention each one deserves. Hence, oversight is given, missed opportunities are maximized and work, productivity, conservation and preservation quality are all less compromised. This approach is seen with the Lord Jesus' handling of His earthly ministry.

25

The Father God gave Him the massive task of building His kingdom on earth comprised of the souls and spirits of redeemed men and women. Broadly stated, that is to build the heretofore, mysterious ecclesia for the Godhead's earthly habitation and enable Creator God to recapture and rule the world with minimal hindrance. Christ's success reauthorizes the Creator who departed the planet in Eden to resume its occupation by His Son whose church as His temple. To do so, Jesus began as His Father began. See Luke 22:29; John 5:17; John 20:21 where Jesus shows him and His Father have been working on this project since before time began.

As the Lord said in John 5:19, 20 and 8:28, His Father taught and showed Him all things and what He learned and saw, He does likewise. What a role model. Keeping with His Father's pattern, Jesus' first official task as the Great Apostle was to segment His commission's duties and distribute them to twelve others. He delegated them portions of His authority as well to assure angels and demons obeyed them. He then dispatched the twelve to help Him spread His message. Luke 6:13 records that of the disciples He called to Himself, Jesus chose twelve and named (titled) them *apostles*. According to this example, titles, then, are meant to inspire trust in another's—often a stranger's—handling of a higher authority's business. Also called agents, delegates may represent their sending principals in legal, judicial, or religious affairs in a distant location.

About Authority

Authority is the lawful right and power to enforce obedience, alter or restrain behavior and conduct by one person or group using the authority of a higher one. Authority is delegated first to positions and becomes attached to the persons that enter them for as long as they occupy it. People enter authority upon being assigned particular jobs or installed in an official post. These explanations say then is that authority is contained within positions, and the titles they are given succinctly describe their work, its scope of duties, range of power, and limits of authority. That these exist prior to the person's entrance into a position says that authority precedes authorization and outlasts it as well.

Authority creates the place where lawful actions and legitimate initiatives and power may be exercised. Leaving any post removes an individual's authority because it was always resident within the office. A person may still wield a considerable amount of influence in a particular sphere upon exiting an office, but legal actions are impossible. An exiting president for example looses the legal authority as a government official to act or enact. Former presidents do however wield considerable influence because of years of service, experience, and the numerous contacts acquired in office.

Otherwise, authority exercised apart from an official position is influence, or anarchy, limited in its ability to lawfully effect change or enforce the rules that govern conduct and behavior. For an influencer to achieve the effects of an authority figure, the influencer must resort to one installed in an office with authority to enact, legislate, or perform what the influencer desires or envisions.

Titles Began Divine

Initially, titles were seen as divine bestowals. The deities of a land, people, or culture gave single terms for the offices they bestowed upon humans appointed to their governments, administrations, military, business, industry, and temples. The pattern clearly shows up in scripture in Yahweh's settlement of Israel and His institution of its government and worship. A nation's deity shortened the numerous tasks, functions, and duties he or she passed on to mortals by naming them in a word after the assigned tasks were explained. The ancient world's deities used titles which connoted the extent of power and authority, privilege and duty, responsibility and accountability delegated from the spiritual world to our natural one. The word *titular*, originally applied to subordinates of divine beings, underscores this as a matter of record. In Bible times, it was accepted that the higher world conferred titular tasks onto their lower worlds as part of the Almighty's heaven to earth protocols. Titles allowed the seen to unseen, divine to human, and immortal to mortal transactions that secured the planet and kept it in eternity's control. If no one else grasps this in today's world, certainly the offspring of the Most High God should.

Titles Back in Time

A worthwhile consideration when attempting to resolve the question of the five-fold and its use of titles is what may be called "the principle of institution." Church leaders constantly wrestle with its ministry titles and offices and how to define its ministers for identification purposes because they do not know where to begin. Efforts to answer the questions typically end in a struggle over action versus being terminology, feeling that what the officers do means more than who and what they are in God's service. Rarely does the simple question of what is the most important factor in their definition enter in, and when it does, it naturally is bogged down in theology. Does the answer of minister authority and officiality rest on function or need, talent or expression? Are the features more important than the officer is, and what language may we use to describe the E-4 staff?

Structure phobia has much of the modern church fearful of order and hierarchy, falling prey to the plight of the proverbial baby and the

27

bath water. Hasty emotional decisions and decrees condemned denominations as bad and detrimental to Christian liberty. This caused protestant leaders and their assemblies to cast off all restraint. "The old was damaging and the new must have no remembrance of it. People do not need leaders in Christ; they need partners. They do not need structure; they need fellowship and freedom. Ministers are not to tell you what to do; they are merely to guide you to the best of your decisions. The congregation is, by virtue of its worldliness, much smarter than the clergy, and functions as the minister's social counselor." Backlash against church domination was extreme, and as seen today, sent God's house and its order in the opposite direction.

In the massive restoration process God's leaders are assigned, a concept that may not have been emerged in those discussions back then is the matter of institutions. Failure to understand what is important to God, or to any founder, in these situations obscures what is most important. What were the founding vision, purposes, and zeitgeist? What determines the organization's endurance? What assures the visionary's standing goals and objectives are achieved and sustained? Are the answers to these questions the people that come and go or the offices that continue after them? Do the people make the office or does the office, title, or position make the person that enters it? To begin to address the issue one must return to organizational protocol and first understand that institutions generally precede their governments and their administration. The offices come before and define the officers. What does this mean?

Founding an Institution

Once people determine to unite in a common purpose under a trusted leader or leaders, the next prudent step in the process becomes government based on some very vital points. The main one is the reason the people were extracted from the rest and connected in the first place. See for scripture guidance, Exodus 19:5; Deuteronomy 14:2; 26:18; Psalm 135:4; Titus 2:14; 1 Peter 2:9. Why did the Godhead, for instance, decree and produce the ecclesia, the called out ones? Deuteronomy 4:5-9 makes the foundation of God's institution clear:

"Behold, I have taught you statutes and judgments, even as the LORD my God commanded me, that ye should do so in the land whither ye go to possess it. Keep therefore and do them; for this is your wisdom and your understanding in the sight of the nations, which shall hear all these statutes, and say, Surely this great nation is a wise and understanding people. For what nation is there so great, who hath God so nigh unto them, as the LORD our God is in all things that we call upon him for? And what nation is there so great,

28

that hath statutes and judgments so righteous as all this law, which I set before you this day? Only take heed to thyself, and keep thy soul diligently, lest thou forget the things which thine eyes have seen, and lest they depart from thy heart all the days of thy life: but teach them thy sons, and thy sons' sons."

After answering this, the ground of perpetual unity is established. Now that the masses are united, what it takes to keep them that way? Nehemiah saw the answer as reinstituting Yahweh's Mosaic Law beginning with the priesthood. Scripture says that the Lord concluded that keeping His church in one mind, heart, and love—His was the only way. These two processes begin to surface and fortify the will of the people.

From here may come some thoughts on how to protect, provide for, and overall secure the people of the community. Doing that begins with understanding what threatens them and undermines their existence. Institutionalizing a populace requires being well versed in what waits to disassemble and destroy them. Then perhaps we would want to discover how they should spend their days and how to ensure that it is prosperous, profitable, and progressive for all concerned. Every member of the community, business, organization, or nation should be rendered productive.

Natural gifts and talents should be perfected for use to better the quality of life for the citizenry. Exchanging these in the form of goods and services sets the stage for the commerce and trade that enriches the group. The institution must help every community get the best out of each one of its citizens individually and collectively and into its society, industry and marketplace. Each capable member's special gifts and talents should be considered part of its human resources and prepared by education and training to meet the needs of the others and vice versa. That means workers. Dwelling and gathering places, special services, food and clothing, education, and worship and all the other aspects of socialization and civilization come into play as the institution anticipates its present and future needs and customs and projects the best means of assuring they are provided beyond the founder's eras. Security and commerce measures assure their gates and borders are safe, and the best interests of the people served without risk to its fundamental purposes. This is crucial, as each generation is responsible for maintaining the institution for the next. Imagine the forethought and insight that requires.

All this is to say that institutions follow their officials only once, in the formative stage. Once it is established, the people fall into its structure and guidelines, government and administration, and the offices dictate their officials. The original vision contains the founder(s) premises. These determine the direction and tenor of the organization and once the institution is founded; the die is pretty much cast. Changes and developments may enlarge the organization, but to override its foundations completely, its originating constitution must be destroyed and a new one instated to accommodate the rise and will of another people.

Officers Staff Institutions

After establishing that they are officers above all else, the next step in the instituting process chain is to recognize what that means. Often, the church defines everything according to itself and its four walls, and what happens on Sunday morning. However, that is not the way the Savior designed or defined His offices to be. He planned His offices' classifications, characteristics, functions, and descriptions for all the needs named and the processes required to see to them must be developed. When all this was done, the offices, their functions defined, the departments described, and the range and lines of authority prescribed, the institution was thus ready to link these to its staff personnel. People with the talents, gifts, experience, and aptitude, along with the interest, are associated with the institutions criteria and departments. The people chosen are tested, interviewed, and screened to see if their gifts, talents, experience, interest, and aptitudes fit what the institution says it requires for employment and/or placement. Those people whose skills, knowledge, and competencies fit what the institution has predetermined it needs are accepted and are place in one of the institution's existing or proposed positions or offices. These are identified by their names that when applied to positions are called titles.

Traditional Church View of Titles

Naively, to date, the traditional church views titles and authority as unnecessary, a view that has done much to dismantle the New Testament church's power and discredit its ministers. Religionists see authority and titles as tools of pride, arrogance, and abuse; as if naming or classifying an official function automatically assures abuse of power. On the other hand, God's perspective and intent for titles and their corresponding authority is to legitimize His involvement and government in human affairs so He does not have to exert His sovereignty on the slightest of human matters. To avoid this, the Lord invests His authority in His designated officials, giving them essential elements of His Creator prerogatives to carry out His will, enforce His righteous laws, and execute His judgments. Apart from titles, those working on the Lord's behalf are stripped of the lawful right to act in God's stead, being devoid of His divine authority to intrude in human affairs. As Jesus' induction of the apostles in the gospels show, especially in Luke 6:13, *title-less* ministers lack the authority they need to override satanic government and act on God's behalf. Confining heaven's eternal law and government to strictly spiritual contexts is a sure way of having the church of Jesus Christ voluntarily abdicate its blood-bought right to impose Creator law and dominion on the kingdoms of men.

The crux of the titles issue is the belief, or at least the rationale, that says titles have the effect of bringing out the worst in people. Besides appearing somewhat juvenile, it subtly conveys the idea that titles, order, law, and government are inherently evil and implies they implant something in a person's heart that was not there previously. The argument is that if ministers do not use titles then Jesus' aim of abject humility is best served. Regardless of how lofty the ideal, there is, as always, another side of the story; the side that points to the Lord. It would seem that if titles were all that culpable the Lord would not have etched their use in His eternal word.

Another point is the Holy Spirit as God moved Paul and the other scripture writers to use titles. Surely, He foreknew the democratic era that would eventually replace the world's long-standing monarchical and imperial ones. As such, would He not see fit to include in His word language that authorized the scriptures to diminish or eliminate as times and trends changed? The fact He did not seems to imply that the Lord meant what He inspired the apostle Paul to write, despite the deterioration of integrity foretold by the apostle in 2 Timothy 3:1-9, which Peter confirmed in 2 Peter 3:3. While there are many synonyms used to downgrade the offices, God had to know that synonyms, while they can certainly affect the spirit or tenor of a document, do not on their own transform its entire intended meaning. So, the words the earlier writers of scripture settled upon best portray the *theo*-monarchical rule of Christ rather than the softened versions selected by today's evangelical democratic society. There is no better place to see this truth at work than when it comes to titles.

Today in our flourishing democratic environment, titles continue to be used in every area of life except in evangelical circles. That is the Spirit-filled, Charismatic, and Word of Faith circles. The Lord's reinstatement of apostles and prophets has brought the conflict to the surface and triggered, in defense of the practice, heated debates as part of traditionalists' campaign against them. It seems during its rise, collectively or individually, title use by Christian leaders was eradicated as a noble display of humility by and between peers and colleagues. However, at present it has shown itself to be disastrous for the body. It was believed the affect that honoring professionals with titles had on church leaders was fueling pride; yet it appears to have boomeranged and perverted Christ's body instead. Church members

31

grew prideful themselves. Becoming spiteful and impudent to its leaders, they ceased to know the ministerial line that separated one from the other. Disrespecting their leadership, they were seduced by familiarity into not heeding or trivializing the Lord's wisdom, righteousness, and counsel, a key part of official ecclesiastical service.

Titles Do Not Infect Hearts—Infected Hearts, But Corrupt Titles &Positions

Blame shifting is a very human response to our embarrassing and infuriating carnal frailties. From Adam's pointing the finger at Eve to her blaming the serpent for her and Adam's fall, the defense still passes on down the line. Historically self-confrontation, a major test of people's maturity and inner integrity, is often failed or avoided. Unfortunately, this adversary crops up again in our question of God's reinstatement of the five-fold, particularly with God's reinstatement of the offices of the apostle and prophet.

Aside from a woeful want of accurate understanding of authority is a church leader's routine disavowal of its source. Renouncing its ministries' status as offices and downgrading the positions into which the Ephesians 4:11 five stand as mere gifts is reflective of naiveté astute professionals normally avoid. In order to redress the problem, one has to come to terms with any struggles they may have with divine authority and the Godhead's authorization of its official functions as delegated to those that carry them out. To adamantly blame the problem of disreputable ministers on semantics, attributing flawed titular activities and misuse of their talents as gifts, is somewhat juvenile. The blame really should be placed where it belongs, on unethical ministers' abuse of the authority and power contained in their offices; anything less dislodges God's authority from His corresponding servants. The reasons for minister abuse need not always be seen as malicious or selfish. For any number of reasons flawed ministers may lack training, be mismatched for their posts, or psycho-emotionally unable to handle the weight of ministry. Whatever the problem, laying blame on titles is plainly shortsighted.

What Comes From Within Defiles

One reliable answer to the situation comes from our Savior's mouth who said that it was not what went into a person that corrupted them but what came out of them (Matthew 15:11). Whatever a person's heart contained upon entering his or her office is what melds with a ministry's power, prestige, and authority. Once in position, a flawed character binds with the office's authority and is wielded by the disreputable soul. The mindset that believes achievement or success equals or rewards with arrogance is tantamount to blame shifting. The truth is that whatever a person credits with his or her success has little to do with its outcomes. Inner vows are more likely the problem, which is what God exposed about Saul whose heart vows were divulged by Samuel the prophet that installed him into kingship. Once what a person inwardly vows is achieved or affected for them to feel "better or above" everyone else, the root of power perversion is sown. Putting such a person in power releases the will to perform the vow, transforming him or her into someone else altogether. Unhealthy emotions that festered along the way to their rise continually gain strength until their vow's outlet through promotion show up.

Settling into a position of power exacerbates ego dysfunctions so that only evil comes out of whatever good the promotion intended. Good or bad leadership are not automatic rewards for success; they are evidence of the motives that drove the success. Titles are merely names that have no power on their own to alter a person's personality, behavior, conduct, or even outlook on life. These surface as the person takes on the duties and responsibilities of the office and its associated pressures. When the office's affects contact the human heart, its inclinations and infections in the character surface.

Calling one's work by its name, identifying or recognizing what it is by what it does, is not of itself corrupt. However, placing one in a position they seek for the purposes of authorizing their natural proclivity to abuse others will energize and empower their inherent hatefulness. It is misleading to suggest that people's disregard or abuse of authority downplays its legitimacy in the body of Christ. The answer to a functional breakdown is not throwing the institution away, but investigating its source and correcting what is malfunctioning. Unfortunately, the typical response of Christians to imperfection is complete *knee-jerk* rejection of everything. Rebuffing God's leaders and their rightful positions only serves to insulate faulty human egos. It is not only deceptive to imply that titles make monsters, but also it puts at discredit those who spread such a notion, and perhaps culpable of denigrating God's divine church order.

The tactic inevitably backfired and a once solid restraint against believer rebellion, disobedience, and overthrow dissolves in succeeding generations. God's people and their societies suffer spiritual backlash from breaking all the Lord's restraints that title laxity, among other things, has much to do with. Today, that is what church leaders face in the wake of the consequences of fostering contempt for God's ordained authorities. Perplexity abounds and ministers as well as leaders in all walks of life struggle to capture Pandora and return her to her box. The church's wisdom and righteousness are shut out of all human spheres as courts, judges, politicians, and social activists all mock it invalid or influential.

Such is the case with the ministers of the New Testament church wrestling with the titles the Lord Himself gave to the Ephesians 4:11 ministers. To claim that what they are called by God to do is irrelevant to who they are is tantamount to saying that God either ceased to exist or fails to influence or tend His church through them. It can also indicate that the church is autonomous and completely free of any obligation to its Lord. Of course, only a few people would voice it that way but the result is still the same. If God thought it was important to name His church officials then He must have had good reason for it. Here we explore some of the Savior's reasons for inspiring His Spirit to communicate the titles to the earth.

To start, we need to shift our concentration from what man believes and would do about leadership, its titles, and ministries if he were God to what the Lord of all creation did and had in mind when He ordained His ecclesiastical offices. Wisdom dictates exploration of what the Creator was treating or responding to in His human spheres when He communicated to Paul the names (titles and offices) He wanted each of His church ministers to be called. Beyond this is what qualified Paul to best comprehend the Lord's mind on those titles. His background on the Sanhedrin prepared him to grasp correctly, what the Lord sought to accomplish through His Corinthian and Ephesian church appointments. All these factors should be carefully considered when attempting to resolve the five-fold, God's divine order, its officers, offices, and their legitimate use of the titles in the church.

The major shift modernists will have to make is how the ancient world saw life and themselves as part of it. Humans were the subordinates and the divine ones were superior. People were the late comers to the planet; its immortal occupants were eternal. Humans were born into the world, and their lot in life its invisible authorities were thought to have prescribed. People died and new ones were born under the control of earth's unseen forces. Consider a consciousness with this view of life and apply your revelations to understanding the scriptures. What insights would you gain into how they would have heard from the heavens, recorded their spiritual and otherworldly encounters, and overall presented and represented their deities?

Lastly, it is also important to relate all the Lord wrote in His word regarding the human experience as God lives it. Humanist rhetoric overlooks the Lord's continual progression to the end times. There is a good reason why Paul understood the redeemed to be hid in Christ, who Himself is hid in God until all things the Father planned are complete (Colossians 3:3, 4). Life goes on because God does not die, not because people will one-day rise again. Thus, the scriptures have more to do with God's life with humanity, His life being lived out through them, than their fleeting existence on the planet. How God

34

keeps a world for subsequent generations to enter, His laws and rules for preserving it and ordering their days on it, and what He saw as essential to maintain His righteousness in the wake of humanist destruction are all noteworthy realities. God's infinite foreknowledge told of the dangers of poor or no recognized leadership as He saw them. Several times in scripture the Lord addresses how humans behave when they view themselves in their own eyes: Deuteronomy 12:8; Judges 17:6; 21:25; Psalm 36:2; and Proverbs 12:15; 16:2; 21:2 are all most significant to our study. This wisdom brought us Paul's officers. Obviously, understanding what the Bible's ministerial names mean to God and how He envisioned those meanings translating to specific church ministries was essential. A serious scholar is duty bound to discover how and what each title means to God and is meant to treat in His church. They should know how the officer's position becomes his or her prosperity. One must also, if he or she believes the Holy Spirit is God, give God credit for being a thinker and recognize that He always uses His foreknowledge of every end from the beginning as the basis for all His decrees and ordinations.

Suggested Activity

What would you write down if you composed a ten-word list defining each officer's title? What would your list contain? How would your terms equate to God's intentions for treating and prospering His church? These are just a few of the many questions that help enlarge your comprehension and appreciation of this material.

In your assignment, conclude with God's plan for His ministers to accomplish and maintain His church individually and collectively as officers. Project the basis of the Lord's estimated qualities and characters, talents and experience for each officer, and you will begin to see what would not work as effectively in one post as it would in another. Apply these questions to all the Ephesians 4:11 officers and answer them in the form of a profile. It just might be that what you write enlarges your insight into the Lord's ministry visions since His is usually the vision easiest to ignore in questions of the church and its doctrine.

Once you have answered the preceding questions or statements of what the Lord foresaw about His church's multi-millennia existence on earth, identify its foes and frustrations, its calling and conflicts in relation to Paul's in Ephesians 4:11 and 1 Corinthians 12:28,29. Express your growth in previous ideas concerning His Ephesians 4:11 positions, apostles and prophets in particular. Show your answers' continued validity in the New Testament church and any difference they may show. Notice any changes in your views or beliefs that you begin to experience and say how it does or does not relate to God's perspective. Talk about, if you agree, how His wisdom makes sense after all.

CHAPTER THREE
A Quick Five-Fold Review

Chapter Topics:

Applying the Term Five-Fold to Christian Ministry • The Five-Fold Hand Analogy in Scripture • The Bible's Hand Imagery • Role and Goal of the Five-Fold Officers • About a Constitution • God's Holy Scriptures Equate to Eternity's Constitutional Government of Earth • Foundation Principles, the Five-Fold Ministry, & Its Doctrines • The Ministry Is Christ's • What Christ's Ministry Consists Of • E-4 Ministry Holds No Personal Prerogatives • The Importance of Profession & Confession in Excellent Ministry • About The Eleven Descriptives • The Minimal Staff of the New Testament Church • 23 Practical Reasons for the Five-Fold • God's Spiritual Equipment for Ministry Service • Know Your Work & the Value of Your Position • Know Your Work Chart

---

N
o significant study of God's divine order in relation to the Ephesians 4:11 officers, classically known in charismatic and evangelical churches as the Five-Fold Offices, would be complete without an appreciation of its foundations. Its foundation, which the apostle Paul discloses in Ephesians, is where it is unveiled for Christ's Church the positions God installed. They were transferred to the New Creation at His ascension to serve Him as long as it remains on earth. In preparation for what we are to cover, we will spend a few moments reviewing them.

The five-fold ministry offices outlined in Ephesians 4:11 are the appointed positions Christ installed in his Body upon his ascension. Having given His disciples the charges of Matthew 28:18-20, Luke 24:44-49, and Mark 15:15-20, He provided them an organized structure within which to carry out His eternal redemptive program. The five-fold ministry offices exist for the express purpose of carrying out for Christ the Mission His Father entrusted to Him, through the church's work on earth.

Applying the Term Five-Fold to Christian Ministry

Aside from the obvious five officers-five fingers connection, the basis for applying the term *five-fold* to New Testament ministry has great merit. Even though in some circles the use of the term is rejected in favor of the term "ascension gifts," the reason for the first appellation warrants further study to see how God's Spirit optimizes its use. While "ascension gifts" too can be rightly applied, the phrase falls short of the Lord's intent in that it implies something that did not exist prior to Christ's return to heaven and subsequent dispatch of His Holy Spirit to birth the church. That is not the case as an understanding of the appellation *five-fold* shows. Its implications deepen our understanding of the church's work and the role of Christian ministry envisioned by God. Although some elements of this discussion appear elsewhere, revisiting its wisdom is helpful in understanding that the ascension gifts operated within God's people before Christ's incarnation, crucifixion, passion and resurrection. The only exceptions are the apostle, if one ignores the *shaliach*, an Old Testament synonym for the apostle, and maybe the evangelist (the herald). Both are discussed later.

The Five-Fold Hand Analogy in Scripture

According to the Old Testament patterns set for us by the Lord, within which the church's ministries are laid, the hand analogy (for five-fold), symbolizing God's ministries, appears to have been deliberate. When one studies the Old Testament word for *hand*, as used for instance in Hosea 12:10, its metaphor forges the synonymous connection with what eventually became New Testament ministry. The Hebrew term used in place of the modern translation for *ministry* is *yad*, meaning *hand*. Among its many other applications is ministry referring to professional service to a sovereign, assembly, nation or deity. The ministry example is repeated throughout scripture several times. In addition to it are the four times the "finger of God" is applied to a work of the Lord through the ministry of His prophets. It appears first in Exodus 8:19, where God through Moses engages Pharaoh and his magicians and sorcerers in a power-over-creation contest. Up to the test of lice, Pharaoh's magicians seem to equal Moses' exercise of the

Almighty's power. The magicians apparently imitated everything Moses did with one exception: they could manifest destruction but were unable to reverse their curses.

With the very first exploit, God shows His superiority and that of His messenger. Moses' serpent ate up the magicians' serpents conjured to compete with Moses' rod. As a case in point, in another instance the adversary could reproduce the plague of frogs but could not command them to disappear. For that, they were forced to appeal to Moses. Such was the case with the plague of lice. Moses was commanded by God to strike the ground and summon all the lice in the area to Egypt to plague man and beast. The magicians, as usual, attempted to duplicate Moses' supernatural feat and then discovered they had reached the end of their magical ability and supernatural authority. Once the lice descended on the land, the magicians recognized that God (referring to the Most High God) had sent the plague and they were powerless to reverse it. They went to Pharaoh, Egypt's king, and admitted that what was done by Moses was done by the *finger* of God.

Later, when Yahweh engraved the Ten Commandments on stone tablets for Moses to govern His new kingdom Israel, the term is used again. This time the Creator's divine legislation is written by the *finger* of God. Twice in this context is the term used (refer to Exodus 31:18 and Deuteronomy 9:10).

The last time the phrase is employed is by our Savior, who declared that He cast out devils by the *finger* of God (see Luke 11:20). God's power was what was energizing His ministry, after God demonstrated His power in Israel. In all the cases where the hand of God was credited with having performed some miraculous feat, it was always witnessed in relation to ministry. The fingers are part of the hand. Thus, the application of the term *five-fold* fits because its use subtly brings forward to the New Testament the Lord's powerful handiwork that made history all along. That same power the Old Testament prophets practiced in their ministries; the very ministries that foretold the Messiah's coming. Hebrews chapter eleven, by the way, is but an abbreviated rehearsal of that historical power at work in earth. Moreover, the practice of God's giving human's visual imagery to foster their comprehension of their Creator is commonplace in Biblical literature. God has always used creation to teach and lead humans to Him unveiling His pragmatic wisdom at the same time. The apostle Paul says it best in Romans 1:20, that the invisible things of God are seen by what is visible.

The Bible's Hand Imagery

The Bible's use of the hand to depict the ministry's work enables perception of God's mechanical operations in earth. The five fingers serve the natural body in the same way the five-fold serves Christ's spiritual body in handling the earth's affairs. The hand displays visually how God executes the offices over which He delegated His Son Jesus authority. It briefly simulates God's maneuvers and earthly manipulations by His church. The functional characteristics shared by the two, the natural hand and the five-fold as God's spiritual hand, are remarkable. Here are a few of their significant similarities. To begin, the human hand is said to contain twenty-seven bones. Interestingly, that number equates to the exact number of books in the New Testament. To continue, the hand grasps, writes, moves, touches, and takes. The palm specifically symbolizes government, supremacy, sovereignty, rulership, and control. The thumb is the opposing power that allows the fingers to grasp and grip, what is required to lift or take hold of something. The thumb is considered the influencer and igniter of subsequent hand movements. The fingers experience sensation, the sensing that enables the hand to hold onto what it grips. Thus, these explanations show how the twenty-seven bones in the human hand further strengthen the link between the hand and Ephesians 4:11 five-fold ministers. The body can function reasonably well with one hand, but not without two. Also, the hand works well with three or four fingers, but it certainly does not perform optimally.

Role and Goal of the Five-Fold Officers

The five-fold ministry officers identify the New Testament Church's authorized ministry officers. Their instatement in the Lord's church incorporates God's blueprint for the planned institution's authority, operations, development, and ministries. Ephesians 4:12-16 illustrates the reasons the officers must exist and the ends to which they serve. Their positions are, as the passage states, Christ appointed and Christ installed. Their aim is to assist Him from eternity in maturing and unifying the Church to abide with Him there forever. With this end in view, Jesus gave His disciples the charges of Matthew 28:18-20, Luke 24:44-49, and Mark 16:15-20, traditionally known as the Gospel Epilogues. Through them, He divulged His plan for the guild of Christian ministry officials to carry out His kingdom business on earth to Paul, whose extensive Sanhedrin experience best qualified him to comprehend the Creator's divine order.

The E-4 officers would serve this purpose and succeed the Lord in the following ways: They would draft church constitutions, dispense and delegate authority, confirm truth, canonize scripture, spot and expose heresy, and formulate policy and plans according to the will of God. These are all after evangelism and conversion succeed. A constitution, by the way, is an organization's form, structure, activities, character, and fundamental rules. Constitution as understood today comes from the Latin word, *constitutio*. It refers to

40

any important law, usually issued by an emperor or other sovereign. The term *constitution* was initially applied in the church to its canon law, its governmental ruling, or decisions relevant to the New Creation. Constitutions assure entities perpetually exist and serve the function for which they were founded despite the life and death cycle that changes its human leaders. Thus, constitutions are concerned with the perpetuity of the organization more than those that enter and leave it.

About a Constitution

An organization is granted its specific powers by a higher authority as long as it abides within its stated constitution or charter. A constitution is a written document that binds everyone connected with an organization, or that which is to become part of it past, present, and future; to its laws, including its monarch; to its chief leaders and prominent members. Constitutions are adopted by an elaborate process called ratification. Its drafters vote on its government, articles and clauses, and sign it into law by those authorized to endorse it. Ratified constitutions coincide with their organization's historical and political perspectives, experiences, and achievements. These generally inspire its formation or alterations to put it into effect.

God's Holy Scriptures Equate to Eternity's Constitutional Government of Earth

The Bible, as ratified by Christ's blood, meets the definition of a constitution completely, up to its government of His New Creation Ecclesia indwelt by the Godhead via the Holy Spirit. Moses' law was to govern the flesh. It served to warn mortals of the dangers of being themselves because of the spiritual infections sin breeds in every human soul. His law intended to provide an alternative to the short life spans that were common to those of the BC era. Humans dying young were not the Creator's will. Isaiah 65:17-20 makes His point:

> "For behold, I create new heavens and a new earth: and the former shall not be remembered, nor come into mind. But be ye glad and rejoice for ever in that which I create: for, behold, I create Jerusalem a rejoicing, and her people a joy. And I will rejoice in Jerusalem, and joy in my people: and the voice of weeping shall be no more heard in her, nor the voice of crying. There shall be no more thence an infant of days, nor an old man that hath not filled his days: for the child shall die an hundred years old; but the

sinner being an hundred years old shall be accursed."

This passage speaks to the new heavens and earth the Lord Jesus caused to appear at Pentecost when His Father's righteousness rained down on earth. Before then, however, while the law was still in effect, He could not halt death. God's love for His people moved Him to delay it, through His Decalogue. The minimum the Lord promised the average person under His domain was eighty years for being righteous. His aim was to eliminate the fear of death that cowered people and led them to succumb to intimidation and compromise to save their lives. The message was simple: "Live by Moses' Law and extend your life." If a person involuntarily failed any one of his laws, they were just to go to the priests and follow their directions to be cleansed and immediately restored.

The Ten Commandments' simple statements divinely legislated human behavior and regulated carnal conduct on the Creator's planet. They work to involve people's will in their life decisions and curtail death's nearly absolute grip. Now people can consent to live to die or to die to live and Romans 5:12-14 makes this point, as does 1 Corinthians 15:22.

God's constitution ratified by Moses provided its citizens with long life and instructions on how to enjoy it prosperously on earth. Jesus' constitution was better because its great provision was eternal life. Differing from Moses' fleshly constitution, His designated divine beings, since it was eternal and governing those who are immortal and cannot experience spiritual death again. Their obligations go beyond the physical behaviors and conduct of the natural man to the everlasting lifestyle of eternal creatures, those in God's family; this is what Ephesians 3:15 mentions. The Savior's constitution aims to select those of the earth most suited to His eternal life and righteous lifestyle. The apostle John alludes to this in 1 John 2:6. The deciding factor is simple: the deemed must resemble Jesus Christ in every spiritual and soulish way; that is what John means when he says that those abiding in Christ ought to walk (live and be occupied with) as He did.

As the eternal Monarch of all creation, the Lord God through Jesus Christ bound Himself to His word and the form of government He instituted in the earth based on what is inscribed in it. Taking the secularist position that the Bible is to change to accommodate societal trends is a dangerous enemy to the scriptures and the redeemed. Limiting its objective to people's development and growth in God rather than God's predetermined transformation of humans is foolhardy. The scriptures are God's definition and production of what He deems a mature human, namely. Ephesians 4:12 is the measure and stature of the Lord Jesus Christ.

Modern Christians should keep in mind that the Bible inscribes God's eternal mind on all His creation. Humanity's dealings with Him are secondary. Its timeliness stems from His revelation of that mind dispensed in specific periods of history and deliberate geographical locations. From before time, from Lucifer and his downfall to the end of time, and to the descent of His mysterious New Jerusalem in John's apocalypse, God's story has unfolded in our physical realm. What this says, then, is that people are born into God's world and are thus obliged to conform to His design of it and them. His culture need not, indeed cannot, be molded around human transience.

People begin life imperfectly, starting out in His world blighted by sin. Sin's darkening of the human soul prevents it from seeing itself by the Creator's light. It takes God's word to tell people that they are dead in trespasses and sins and were born spiritually dead; that is, alienated from the Creator's life and light. God's righteousness because of this has no place in them. It is only when the lost soul confronts himself or herself in the light of God's truth that the sin that was once so natural to the carnal being is seen for what it is: exceedingly sinful and painful. God's answer to human sinfulness is not merely a matter of needing to be born again, but it also encompasses being purged from all the worldly influences and genetic inferiorities the sin nature embedded in the human consciousness. For these reasons, it is ludicrous to think that scripture should be, or even can accurately be, reinterpreted to fit the discoveries and trends of emerging generations. The idea overlooks the reality that modernism and its technology do not remedy sin. It only provides more efficient and pervasive ways for the same old human nature to execute its sin. Take the following facts as examples.

Today's modern devices are just as helpful to the sinner as they are to the saint. For instance, telephones rush gossip (a human compulsion) to hungry ears in seconds. Television speeds pornography (perversion of godly pleasures) to the lusty soul. Motorized vehicles accelerate criminals' transportation from place to place, and electronic media whisks billions of evil and good thoughts throughout the world in an instant. All sorts of technological and medicinal devises retard the consequences of sexual sins while counteractive drugs hide or delay its deadly affects. Advanced printing technologies hasten the devilish fantasies that seduce the soul to sin and on it goes. Technological devices promote and serve or deter and hinder human vices. You see the problems the Lord addresses in His world through scripture relate to His righteousness that is unfathomable to the unregenerate soul. God's declaration that no human is born with or understands righteousness apart from His truth vindicates it.

God is dealing with the inherent drive all people share to lie, steal, kill, and destroy; their obsession to pervert truth and despise the Creator without knowing why. God's word addresses these issues from eternity eons before the earth was formed and the world as we know was made. Sin is not a coeval matter that varies with each generation. Human intelligence or innovation does not affect it because it is a drive, an obsession, a compulsion. Sin does not begin with what people do, but with what they want and feel the need to do. That is what the Savior means by what he says in Matthew 15:18-20. Applying the scriptures with these eternal motivations in mind will more than caution future generations and their scholars against tampering with the Godhead's everlasting constitution.

As ministers of Christ, His five-fold cabinet would mold and execute the Church's constitutional mandates exercising their divine authority to authenticate its missions and verifying its doctrines and upholding its observances. The officers, in addition, identify and develop those to assist and succeed them in the Lord's perpetually expanding kingdom, stabilizing it as they constantly construct and conform each generation to its content.

As their generations came and went, the Ephesians 4:11 staff of successors would reconstruct the ministerial fabric of God's kingdom throughout the world in every era of humanity affecting all stratum of earthy life. Overall, the five ministry officers would continually carry out Christ's governmental program for the mission His Father entrusted to Him. From God's perspective, they are to serve for the duration of the Church Age, establishing, nurturing, overseeing and guarding (that is keeping and protecting) Christ's Bride as long as she remains on earth. The sum of Ephesians 4:12-16 declares these as the underlying objectives of their work. Although the names and faces change from era to era, the ordinations of the institution called the "ecclesia" continue. As long as it remains, the need for the five-fold offices named by Paul as standing positions awaits those ordained to fill them.

Foundation Principles, the Five-Fold Ministry, & Its Doctrines

Integral to the aforementioned epilogues of the three gospels (another name for closing sayings of Christ in the gospels) are eleven descriptives that may explain and direct the originating and sustaining efforts of the five-fold in His church. Studying them shows they perfectly describe the work the Church engages in consistently to occupy itself until the Savior returns. These descriptives may be seen as job descriptions that standardize the Lord's ministerial guidelines for ecclesiastical service. Those occupying the Ephesians 4:11 offices can see their service to God in action as follows:

- Preach the Gospel
- Make Disciples
- Baptize Disciples
- Teach Disciples
- Heal the Sick
- Motivate Salvation's Repentance
- Inspire Disciple Sanctification
- Qualify Disciples to Receive Inheritance
- Equip Disciples for Ministry
- Train Disciples for Ministry
- Prepare Disciples for Eternal Life

The Ministry Is Christ's

For today's ministers to become as effective and reliable to God as their predecessors, it should be remembered that the ministry with its offices and operations is born Christ's. Recalling earlier discussions about principals, Christ's Father gave the ecclesiastical mission and its subsequent ministries to Him upon His ascension and return to eternity's throne. As Ephesians 4:7, 8 will tell you, Jesus in turn "gave gifts to men," as foretold in Psalm 68. Christ gave to those who entered His kingdom gifts of services that allow them to take part in His ongoing mission and work. Based on this information, it is erroneous to claim personal prerogatives over the ministries the Lord gives. Those occupying the Ephesians 4:11 (E-4) positions are but helpers and co-laborers to Him in His effort to restore humanity to life. Effectively performed they become the means by which the Savior redeems us back to His Father God.

What Christ's Ministry Consists Of

Christ's ministry consists of more than witnessing to one's family and associates or sharing one's testimony. It also involves more than gathering a few people to start a church or preaching to whoever will hear. Success in Christian ministry begins with being declared throughout eternity and eventually the world as being approved unto God. The Lord Jesus, our example, was faced with countless opportunities to pander to the praise of people, and without question had numerous occasions to abuse His divine power and authority. Considering the hostility He faced routinely, He could have at any given point in time rashly declared Himself king and, seizing the reins of this world's government, avenged and defended Himself. In fact on one such occasion, He had to escape the clutches of earthly kingmakers to prevent them from forcibly making Him Israel's king out of season: "*When Jesus therefore perceived that they would come and take him by force, to make him a king, he departed again into a mountain himself alone,*" (John 6:15). The passage provides great wisdom and insight to the one who would serve Christ today. Doing so with integrity includes executing ministry positions, what the call to ministry encompasses, understanding it is much more than sermonizing.

Achieving the Godhead's ends requires true ministers to be open to the Holy Spirit's diverse gifts, different ministries, various activities or operations as stated in 1 Corinthians 12:2,3. Furthermore, the Lord's purposes for the church should be well understood. Every minister ought to remember that whatever the Lord does is always to *manifest Himself as the living God by the Holy Spirit.* When God dispenses His graces for our services and the different privileges, honors and authority that go with them, they are to distribute the powerful resources needed for humans to get His assigned jobs. His bestowals are always according to the counsel of His will and His creator foreknowledge of His handiwork.

The Lord's dispensations, another word for economy, stewardship or management, are dispersed based on who we are, how we are made, and what we were made (and saved) to do. Nevertheless, the power wielded in God's service, as Paul and the other church founders discovered, is His and not the ministers. It is to glorify Himself and His Son, not us. That His ministers enjoy a portion of that glory too speaks to God's greatness and demonstrates His distaste for mediocrity or impotence in those indwelt by Him. God's liberal sharing of His great strength compensates for what would ordinarily cause us to fail in His service. The Lord's tiniest strength delivers potency to His people that undoubtedly reverberates with honor, glory, and awe toward those who serve Him in the earth.

E-4 Ministry Holds No Personal Prerogatives

Today there is the penchant of modern ministers to claim personal prerogatives over the gifts and callings they receive for God's service. Often ministers say, sometimes brag, that they have the gift of such-and-such or that their ministry is thus-and-what. Though not inherently wrong if communicated in the right spirit, such as that of an assignment rather than a possession, the practice can be dangerous. In the wrong mouth or ears, it can breed the temptation to presume upon the Lord's divine purpose for personal advantage. Doing so can lead naive or errant ministers to impose their will on the work the Lord actually delegated, thus fulfilling their dreams or fantasies in the guise of a God-given vision. To be effective in ministry, the first thing ministers know from God's grooming over the decade or so of preparation it took to ascend to an office is that New Creation ministries—*everyone's*—are Christ's. They constitute the substances of His commission received from the Father. The entirety of the Christian ministry originates and emanates from the Lord Jesus Christ. In assigning its ministries, God delegated His New Testament ecclesia everything it was to do exclusively on His behalf and at His behest. There is no such thing as a personal claim or private stake in the New Testament church's ministries. All that God calls anyone to do is but a sub-portion of the original work that brought Jesus to earth in the first place. Everything Christ's servants do extends His original work in the world to be performed throughout all ages. That premise makes ministry an all-encompassing duty assigned to predesignated individuals throughout the millennia of the church's existence.

For example, when the Son of God came to earth He was alone in His endeavor to call out a people for God. See Isaiah 50-55 and 42-45. Before His appearance on the religious front of the Roman era, the idea of Yahweh being anything more than the God of the Jews, with a Son on top of that, was non-existent. Of the many gods, none of them really produced or exhibited, although they purported to do so, a founder with the unquestionable powers and authority of a faithful serving deity. Jesus, according to history, was the first one to do so. One encounter with Him established that His was no mere mortal Servant of wizardry or sorcery. Being raised outside religious circles, Jesus was ungroomed by human hands. Consequently, He taught outside the religious training institutions of His day, exceeding their knowledge by aeons.

Our Savior had no followers, no helpers, no possessions, nor ministers when He began; this was the characteristic nature required of apostleship put upon Him. The Savior, to do His work and fulfill His Father's command, was to start by discovering those that His God assigned Him and convert them to His mission, His second priority. The first one was that He present Himself to those whom He was sent and introduce them to His unusual message. What a powerful and weighty calling. These activities launched the Lord Jesus' professional ministry.

The Importance of Profession & Confession in Excellent Ministry

Ministry is a profession, even if salvation is a matter of the convert's confession. The distinctive between the two terms is more important for ministers to grasp. Frequently, interpreters of the numerous New Testament's translations in the book of Hebrews render the word *profession* in the passage as simply a confession. However, the latter term, *confession*, centers mainly on the saying (verbalizing) aspects of Christianity, seeming to isolate its words of conviction from their corresponding works. The word *profession*, on the other hand, though it includes inferences of the word *confession*, takes divine intent further than just saying whom one is and what one believes, distinguishing the two by setting one above the other for the purposes of object and outcome. To use the word *confession* is to say or declare something motivated by an inward vow. It means, "to avow a belief, promise, etc." To *profess* something, on the other hand, is to extend that avowal to a call to work or a vocational occupation.

Thus, the writer of Hebrews 3:1 sought to expand the ordinary (and perhaps initial) perception of the convert's *confession* to encompass a corresponding work by which the vow may be recognized in action. In that context, the Lord Jesus served the Almighty as His official agent, a minister, and officer of His Father's church. The profession-confession idea is fully presented in the language of James 1:23-25. It seeks to convey that redemption is not merely a matter of saying, confessing, and avowing. Rather it extends to working outwardly, what one is saying in order to prove the sincerity of the vow. Subsequently, to confess and profess both intend "a vow made to Christ" witnessed by subsequent lifestyle changes emanating from the faith that inspired the vow. Together, the two correlate to what constitutes a living conversion to the Son of God.

About The Eleven Descriptives

What this discussion calls the *Eleven Descriptions* represents Christ's ministry program and its aims as handed down by His Father God. Anyone seeking to serve them should become intimately familiar with every aim in order to do their part in bringing them to pass on Christ's behalf. If studied carefully one would see these descriptives disclose Christ's ministry works and reflect the ambassadorial responsibilities He ordains. We concentrate as we go through our study of the E-4 Ministries on this work, the process, and the object of these positions. From this material, you will come to understand God's "big picture" for these offices. Once enlightened, you will see what makes E-4 ministries the *vital instruments* of His vision: to God they are *instruments*, even if to humanity they are gifts.

48

The Minimal Staff of the New Testament Church

God, according to our Ephesians and Corinthians scriptures, ordained His churches (those established and shepherded by his Son Jesus Christ under the ministry of His Holy Spirit) are to be staffed with nothing less than apostles, prophets, and teachers. He further ordained they be endued with supernatural powers and efficacy endowments to facilitate the offices' mission, strengthening those who fill His church offices as long as it remains on the earth. What makes theirs a perpetual assignment is God's pragmatic acceptance of the inevitable weaknesses of the flesh? He knows that as long as sin, Satan, God, and man all remain the same—sin in man, man in darkness, and God immutable—the need for the E-4 ordinations continue. For these reasons, what the early church leaders and founders inscribed as the Lord's ordinations remains unchanged today in God's mind. His wisdom dictates that the Church, the body of Christ at large, is to be protected by these supernatural dispensations worldwide. Its officers busily handle God's kingdom officiations as Christ's Bride's ongoing global assignment. Following are examples:

1. Evangelizing and discipling the world

2. Continuance of the truth

3. Growth, sanctification, and holiness

4. Maintenance of supernatural strength

5. Preservation of purity, wholeness, soundness, and overall well-being

6. Equipping for service

7. Preparation for ministry duty

8. Maturation for eternal existence

9. Increasing the flock in the knowledge of God

10. Stability of the faith

11. Knowledgeable interaction and communion with the Godhead

All the above qualities and traits fall under this umbrella of Divine Order in the broadest possible sense. Below are twenty-three specific reasons the Lord installed and continues to need His five-fold officers. Studying each one on its own merits and attaching practical activities to them easily enlarges one's perception of these officers and their value to the church.

23 Practical Reasons for the Five-Fold

God ordained His ministries to perform and accomplish specific things for Him in His church and throughout the world. Continually, they are to do the following:

1. Preach Christ's Gospel
2. Make Disciples, Who Become God's Sons and Daughters
3. Baptize Christ's Disciples into His Word and Spirit
4. Teach Disciples
5. Heal the Sick
6. Deliver Captives
7. Motivate Repentance
8. Inspire Sanctification
9. Qualify Heirs for Blessings
10. Equip for Service
11. Train for Ministry
12. Appoint Ministers
13. Install Ministers
14. Oversee Ministers
15. Execute God's Will/Plan
16. Officiate God's Affairs
17. Impart Spiritual Gifts
18. Perform the Supernatural
19. Promote Holiness
20. Ready Church for Eternal Life
21. Keep Christ the Center of the Faith
22. Enable Fellowship with the Godhead

23. Enable Submission to Leadership & Government of Holy Spirit

God's Spiritual Equipment for Ministry Service

Before anything, know and understand the following conditions for faithful, diligent service to the true and living God! Below are thirty-five expressions that indicate one is a qualified or effectual minister of Christ's gospel. Although they are mainly intangible, they are needed to represent Christ righteously before His sheep and to the world. The thirty-five expressions, also known as spiritual equipment, are the best way for people not to become disillusioned with their ministers and Christian leaders. For instance, how often have you heard it said that reverend, apostle, prophet, or pastor so-and-so was gifted, very charismatic, but lacked character? How frequently have you heard that some church member or follower was wounded by an especially popular and anointed minister whose lifestyle and private conduct failed to live up to doctrine?

The answer to such a disparity is that the minister ably emulates what aspirers have observed over time. Many of them just assumed themselves a Christian minister without having a real encounter with the Lord Jesus Christ. They so mimic their favorite pastor or speaker, their own personalities and identities disappear. This common occurrence can be relied on to help locate where a professing servant of God stands with Him. They help the saint gauge the nature and condition of his or her fruit in His service. To be a quality representative for the Lord, you must possess and experience these:

1. Love for God

2. Commitment to holiness

3. Zeal for God's righteousness

4. Apprehension of divine truth

5. Acceptance of humanity's universal sin

6. Realization of sin in the flesh

7. Understand flock's need for maturation

8. Recognize need for all mankind to repent and be saved

9. Allegiance to God

10. Determination to uphold God's truth

11. Willingness to rebuke/warn of sin's judgment

12. Self-sacrifice and loss of identity

13. Obedience/submission/surrender

51

14. Proper God-approved training

15. Able to nurture and train the flock of God

16. Peculiar human insight

17. Strength of conviction

18. Defensive about the gospel

19. Protective of God's kingdom

20. Zealous safeguard of God's sheep

21. Hungry for God's company

22. Reverence for God's sovereignty

23. Respect for God's judgments

24. Little regard for the world

25. Contempt for worldliness

26. Longing for heavenly home

27. Aching for God's lost sheep

28. Certainty of final judgment

29. Eager to see the end of this age

30. Need for continuous fellowship with God

31. Strong sense of duty

32. See gravity of the office

33. Know scope of responsibility

34. Know full impact of office demands and influence

35. Comprehend outcome of efforts and work

These characterizations enable the serious servant to not only answer his or her call, but they act as the impetus he or she needs to succeed in the call's labors.

Know Your Work & the Value of Your Position

Often people entering God's ministry do so on zeal alone. They have had a special encounter with the Lord, some revelation, and a passionate sense of being called to preach, which is how most of them phrase the call. Others may say that they were told by the Lord to start a church. However way it is stated, the initial result is the same.

People that have sat in church mesmerized by an especially charismatic minister watch how their view of ministry is done for a while. When they feel they have seen enough, they often launch out on their own prematurely, perceiving it to be easy and trouble free. In their fantastical minds, they can do that; after all, what does it take to get a place for some singing or a pulpit to preach? Maybe they include some counseling, hold a prayer line and some special meetings, but overall how hard can it be? It is that attitude that sets new ministers and their ministries up for culture shock. Despite all the spiritual rhetoric they may have absorbed to the contrary, the church world is a culture. When one enters it, he or she meets a myriad of rules, signals, and codes often unspoken and somewhat vague that can determine the minister's eventual success or failure.

This material is to widen the minister's sights and anticipations of ministry. The chart below categorizes Christ's ministry work program to help you approach His work with a more definitive mind. Doing so enables Christ's ministers to project their outcomes and more accurately measure their success in His service. The idea of measurements is often disdained by evangelical, word, charismatic, and pentecostal churches. However, they are valuable to those that desire to evaluate their success and integrity in God's service. Measurements provide a true yardstick by which to judge the fruits of Christian labors. They permit right self-assessment in comparison with God's measurements and equate to Ephesians 4:12 and 13 outcomes of a saint grown into the "measure and stature of Christ's fullness."

Know Your Work Chart
How It All Starts

Evangelism
Revival
Discipling

From these core activities come the ongoing process of transforming converts into disciples and disciples into sons (and daughters) of God, His divine offspring if you will.

~~~~~~

The Disciple to Sonship Process

It is based on Ephesians 4:12-16; Romans chapter 8 (specifically verse 30); Romans 15:16; Galatians 5:19; 22-24; and Ephesians 1:1-5:32. It is recommended that students complete a Topical Scripture Study of all terms, separately and collectively, for potential class discussion as applicable.

Inspiration	**Indoctrination**	**Sanctification**	**Resurrection**
Organization	**Motivation**	**Preservation**	**Glorification**
Revelation	**Edification**	**Liberation**	
Stabilization	**Application**	**Dedication**	

CHAPTER FOUR

Gift vs. Office Mentality

Chapter Topics:

Public Office, Private Devotions, Public Ministry • Theology & Doctrine • Problem with Gift-Only Mentality • Contemplations for the Gift-Only View of Ministry • A God View of the Church's Offices: God Does Not Fear Power, His nor Ours • God's Kingdom is Spirit: The Church Joins Forces with the Heavens • The Ecclesia • Confirming Ecclesiastical Citizenship

---

I n this chapter, we discuss how an office surpasses a mere activity, what exercising a gift primarily or initially entails. The aim is to provide sound wisdom for understanding the value and status of an office over the generally casual though occasionally influential practice of a gift.

A quality educational training program does two necessary things. It educates and trains. Using well defined goals, objectives and outcomes, it declares what it sets out to do, accomplishes it, and then informs the student how to recognize its accomplishment in them upon completion. Every one's objective, through its chosen materials, is to speak to what learners need to understand and perform adequately in their chosen fields of study. Ideal learning material should tackle the strengths and weaknesses of its field, including its proponents and opponents, what people respond to most or dislike about it, and how the learner may counter, conquer, or override their opposition. These may be competitors with equal or similar strengths and values or former leaders in the field that have not kept up as they should with changing trends and user or consumer needs and views. At the least, these should motivate learning and teaching programs that study God's ministries.

Public Office, Private Devotions, Public Ministry

Often the question is asked, "Should one occupy or be installed in an office to carry out every ministerial activity assigned by the Holy Spirit?" The question arises because frequently there is dispute when leaders require certain ministries to be officially recognized before permitting them to function in the church. The answer rests on whether a person is practicing a gift normally exercised in private settings, such as devotions, or executing an office in public ministry. When asked this question, I usually respond by saying that you do not need to be in an office to pray for others or to intercede, for example. Usually the validity and biblicity of the intercessor's office is brought into question. I say that intercession may be conducted and accomplished on the merits of one's devotional life with the Lord, as can all spiritual activities. Private devotions and personal prayer are sufficient for the Spirit to tell a worshipper to pray for (or help) this or that one. Relationship alone is enough to share with the object of one's intercession what the Lord says in response. If the intercessor knows the person or can relate to him or her in any credible way, he or she will be open to discuss and hear what "thus says the Lord" as spoken to the intercessor about him or her in prayer. It characterizes a casual ministry and may be quite effective. It is, however, insufficient for public ministry.

The church is an institution; organic or organizational, it functions as an institution. That means, for those desiring or having a ministry call to be recognized by it, to be respected and allowed to officially function within it, they must do so on the basis of a public ministry and not the fruit of private, generally unsubstantiated or unverifiable experiences with the Lord. *Officially* here means with the recognition and authorized backing of its leadership. Much of the debate over the matter has to do with people's wanting to impose private prayer responses and revelation on the wider body of Christ as a public minister. Without legitimate status, preparation, and acknowledgement, they seek to be regarded as an authorized dispatch representative of their messages from God. As an official minister, they want to publicize what God releases to them as a son or daughter.

Far too often, major campaigns are launched on devotional revelations that have no more far-reaching intent by God than answered prayer. Books are written, slogans are tagged, and mottos propagated from what Christians receive from the Lord for themselves. Personal wisdom and counsel are dispensed as instructions, guidelines, or practices for public ministry and herein lies the gist of controversy. Seasoned ministers know the sound and tenor of private and devotional interactions with the Lord. They know what should remain in the prayer closet because its application is too narrow or situational for the broader body of Christ. They comprehend what will be greedily received, spark a dangerous frenzy, and in the long run overthrow sound doctrine and established biblical truth. Many of them make the decision to conceal something wonderful and explosive the Lord released to them in worship because inwardly they knew it to be manna for their circumstances, but potentially or ultimately dangerous to the church at large. This example answers how simple slogans become theological and doctrinal mania. What should have remained in a person's journal or diary recklessly made its way to center stage purely on the ground of novelty.

Sincere ministers always use Ephesians 4:12-16, 5:10; 2 Timothy 3:16; Romans 15:4 and 1 Corinthians 10, which share the admonishment to include all scripture and use it to confirm all revelation. Sound doctrine, wisdom, and outcome (fruit) measure what God expects His ministers to use to assess truth and gauge what is or is not "what His Spirit is saying to the churches." The index has to be how the person got the word, the circumstances under which it was received, and how it related to those circumstances. The acid test is what happens when the word is applied. Does the matter brought before the Lord that released the revelation pertain to His church worldwide? Generally, passages received from God as a response to a petition are restricted in their application. They may fit several Christian's circumstances and still have no practical benefit to the body.

Nine times out of ten, this pattern depicts the private devotions that should not be dispensed as public manna. Self motivations rarely make good grounds for objective revelation. Usually, God's revelations, when meant for public ministry, come because of His own initiative. He typically gets His ministers thinking on a matter or brings one to their attention that concerns Him that has become widespread. As His ministers begin to study the subject at His unction, God proceeds to reveal His mind on it and directs them to several passages of scripture that support His revealed thoughts. That is how messages for public ministry are routinely delivered by the Lord.

Theology & Doctrine

Among the numerous rivals to the Lord's reinstatement of the entire E-4 offices are doctrine and theology. The doctrine of pastors as supreme church rulers is covered elsewhere. However, another effective tactic that confuses the matter is that of ministry positions being merely gifts and not necessarily offices. Most teachers and leaders of the preceding move demote all the church positions to mere giftings to weaken the authority that abides in the offices. A presumed aim for doing so appears to be so that no one office is seen as more important or significant than the others are.

Interestingly, the only office to escape this tactic is the pastorate. Otherwise, the rest, especially the apostle and prophet, are confined to the limits of gift nomenclature. For example, when people think of apostleship, they are unprepared to consider the office as the Lord ordained it and often flagrantly rebel against it, subtly despising divine order and scripture authority in the process. Their reaction stems from an inbred theological fear.

Many Christians upon encountering apostleship are terrified of what they have been told it represents: rigid authority, haughty power-hungry leaders, and money-grubbing elites that live only to suck the life and prosperity out of their followers. Others are fearful of being forced to change their lifestyles, become (legalistically) holy, and feel compelled to get too spiritual. Still more dread apostleship because its doctrine is perceived to be too deep and mystical, while another group may just despise the idea of anything striking ecclesiastical hierarchy. However, anything that restrains by fear leads to religious bondage. It just may be that the very liberal superficiality that tags apostleship as legalism and overly religious may itself be guilty of the same thing. In any event, the purpose of this discussion is to show that the ministers in 1 Corinthians 12:28, 29 and Ephesians 4:11 are more than performance giftings or charismatic acts, they are officials of the Godhead's ecclesia.

Problem with Gift-Only Mentality

The problem with the gift over office belief is that people do what they want with gifts. They keep them, stuff them in closets, toss them, or give them away. As a rule, people rarely view a gift as essential unless it serves their personal needs. When a recipient no longer sees any good use for a gift, it is generally mistreated or discarded, and that is what happened to Christ's ministry offices. The church diminishes official ministry authority by classifying all servants as gifts to the body. Doing so emphasizes the talents and charisma they display over their legitimate call to God's authority. This whittles down their capacity to enforce obedience to God and His way of life and enables Christians' rebellion, intended or not, as understood by the apostle Paul in Romans 15:18: "For I will not dare to speak of any of those things which Christ hath not wrought by me, to make the Gentiles obedient, by word and deed." *Obedient* there means to hearken and heed, attend to, comply with, and submit to. These are the Lord's goals for His ministry offices.

Downgrading the ***diakonia*** (persons in offices) to ***charisma*** (people exercising their gifts) was a shrewd coup on Satan's part. It effectively eliminated his competition for power and authority over humanity and its spheres. The success of this coup is seen in the church's loss of serious influence in world affairs. It is routinely ignored and precluded from every major aspect of human life. The Christian Church is now no more than a ceremonial center to christen babies, baptize penitents, marry people, and conduct funerals. Outside these, the typical person sees no reason to regard the church, and most of them joke about attending it only for weddings and funerals.

Of all God's seven spheres of creation, none is dominated by the New Creation church. In contrast, though, all the false religions, idols, and humanism of the world and ministers have established strongholds in the world's high places. Freely, they are empowered to peddle their messages, release their demonics, and overall pervert the world's spiritual climate with their philosophy and ideology. The authority the church once wielded in the world is gravely diminished by those who lost sight of its original purpose (see Lamentations 1:9, NKJV) in the world as its light, salt, wisdom, and truth; the only way to the Creator.

Any meager influence the church holds in the name and power of Jesus Christ is done so by what the world calls evangelicals, establishing the spirit of the evangelist's as the dominant control of any religious power Christ presently retains. While evangelicals are mega, they still gave us the impotent Christianity seen today. There is a natural truth that those who only bring children into the world (midwives for instance) deliver only babies. Parents on the other hand produce stable mature adults. The reality holds true on the spiritual front as well. Scripture emphatically says the New Creation is nurtured and stabilized by the apostles' doctrine, signs, wonders, miracles, and government. The absence of their mantles from mainstream Christian ministry left the task of rearing the family in the sphere of midwifery.

Historically, compromise, tolerance, and syncretism flourish in such a climate. Society's comfortable co-existence and praise of the evangelicals attests to it. Many members of these churches barely know right from wrong, Jesus from the antichrist, and God from the devil. Often they cannot fathom the Creator's holiness, justice, or righteousness and the Bible's interpretation is up for grabs. All these conditions cause sinners to ridicule Christ's sacrifice and the church to abdicate His kingdom's government in the world. Frustrating the Lord's authority in the realms and spheres of men and minimizing His awesome power at work in the church, Christian ministry exploits are reduced to mere parlor tricks that entertain but fail to sustain.

The outcome is the result of God's wisdom being severed from His works. Mature godly ministers understand the foolhardiness of weakening the Lord's hold on His planet and His body and would readily present and promote the authority, order, and government of an office rather than the free exercise of one's gift. Theirs is a breakthrough mentality that the modern church's mind worldwide must embrace. Titles serve God's purposes better than gifts because authority is needed before actions can be legitimately undertaken or before they become beneficial to anyone concerned.

Contemplations for the Gift-Only View of Ministry

The gift-only application frees church ministers to engage in and perform their ministries at will, and according to their own discretion. Such a loose definition requires little thought be given to the official purposes God intended for His ministers or their outcomes. God's eternal motivations for installing them in His church are hardly a factor in how one exercises his or her ministry gift.

Moreover, the gift mentality ignores the Lord's job descriptions, official duties, and His operational guidelines for each individual office. What this does is encourage intrusions into another's sphere, often to the ministry's detriment. However, to resolve the matter according to our Lord's satisfaction and achieve His desired aims, God's specific designs must be discovered and understood. Some critical questions should be asked that include, "Why did God inspire the apostle Paul to write 1 Corinthians 12:28, 29 and Ephesians 4:11 despite humanity's natural penchant for rebelling against authority? What heavenly and human visions and outcomes made them so important to Him in the first place? What spiritual climate are these offices to set by occupying their posts and the type of produce they should yield on earth considering Ephesians 3:10? Could you answer how God's earthly agents are to cooperate with His invisible order and say what exactly divine order looks like and accomplishes? Can you now say what about the E-4 staff, in God's mind, makes the E-4 perpetual and mandatory?

All church ministers should be able to say how the Lord's eternal wisdom is to be used to structure His church and cover His world, and identify specific scripture patterns to support their responses. For instance, how quickly and articulately can you say what Jesus envisioned for His body on earth before time began? Can you make outsiders understand the basis of God's divine order in the first place? If you were part of a discussion panel, could you honestly relate how we got this way in the church and put forth plausible suggestions and solutions to the most expedient paths to restoring the Bible's model?

A God View of the Church's Offices: God Does Not Fear Power, His nor Ours

Unless there is an apprehension of the Lord's communication that of heaven to earth instead of the typical man to God perspective, humanity's mindset on the matter will never be settled. Since ministers are agents of their senders, it is impossible for the one sent to alter the sender's intensions, not to mention how anarchic it is. In Bible times, only those with private aims and selfish ambitions would consider doing so.

In relation to our subject, the Lord of glory has good reasons for inspiring Paul to write "first apostles, secondarily prophets, and thirdly teachers" as His church appointments. Much debate and discussion has raged on the subject as error, archaic mindsets, and primitive tyrannical thinking have all made the truth hard to accept. It is difficult to fathom that the Lord, the God of love, would impose upon us such a rigid unchangeable order of staff ministers over His church. Independent liberal mentalities cannot imagine the Creator not comprehending the age-old adage that "power corrupts and absolute power corrupts absolutely." This subtle influence consistently undermines divine order and paves the way for Christians to reject God's granting any human authority over another, even if it is godly authority. Yet they live and expect it from secular authorities.

Human's wrestle with the reality that what frightens them does not terrify God. He sees and calls the end of everything from its beginning. God does not fear human or earthly powers and repeatedly demonstrates His dominion over His creatures worldwide. The Lord also does not fear losing control of His creation or of those He puts in power. He recognizes that all flesh is as grass and returns to the dust. In the afterlife, they fall into His hands. That He is able to remove them from the earth in an instant keeps His power preeminent in all affairs.

The monarchical era of the Bible's development, having given way to modern democracy, assumes that the Lord shares humanity's difficulty with His church's leadership and authority being delegated to humans. To act on their fear, they responded by replacing it with a strictly lateral church government structure. The prevailing belief is that either the Lord entrusts His ecclesiastical authority to the entire body equally based on each member's personal sanctions, or He nullified it altogether. However, when discussing God's divine order regarding the five-fold ministries (or ascension gifts, as some would call them), aside from respecting God's founding principals for the offices, one must take care not to impose their pet religious phobias on His wisdom. While it is prudent to be guided by the church's historical leadership record when considering those to stand in its ministry offices or reacting to those who enter it, the fact remains that God's design serves enduring purposes. He devised functions that transform His body into what it must become to survive and thrive in eternity, ordaining that we fulfill His Son's ministry as the Godhead envisioned. God's ministers are not to baby-sit, but are instead to nurture and settle His body in conformance to His plan for its eternal reign and service. Grasping God's reasoning for the apostle and prophet as the church's foundation ministers calls for more than personal experiences or historical records. It requires the seeker to start with faith in the Lord's omniscient wisdom and commitment to His eternal purview of the human experience and involvement in church and world events.

God's Kingdom is Spirit: The Church Joins Forces with the Heavens

The one Bible text replete with apostolic wisdom and insight is Paul's epistle to the Ephesians. It refers to the church's earthly connection with the heavens four times. Paul's revelation no doubt recalls Jesus' words in Matthew 16:19 where He promised that our authority as His ecclesia would enjoy the zenith of its powers from the heavens to earth. God's church, says Ephesians 1:3, receives its blessings from heavenly places. In addition, it is to those heavenly places that God the Father elevated His Son Jesus, the New Creation church's founder. Furthermore, Ephesians 2:6 adds that we, His body, were also raised to those same heavenly places to sit together with our Lord and Savior Jesus Christ.

Beyond all this, Ephesians 3:10 lets us know that we are not heaven-seated anonymously or impotently because it says that the principalities and powers in heavenly places are shown God's manifold wisdom by the church—that would be us. That is not all, because the church's primary and most enduring messengers are not human but divine; they are the seven angels of the seven churches introduced to the apostle John on Patmos.

Lastly and most importantly, the church will spend eternity together with Jesus Christ, the Son of Man. He is not a president, an elected official presiding over many, but a king. God's is a theocracy and no amount of trendy rhetoric or refusal to acknowledge it will change the fact. While earthly kings may have done their share to blight the idea of kingship, in particular divine kingship, the truth is that the New Creation ecclesia is being prepared to reign as sub-regnants under a king. That is why God needs no additional texts or revelations to enlarge His scripture.

It was in no way an accident that the Lord chose to end His canonical transmission to the world while king's still reigned. So confident of this was the Savior that when He inspired the apostle John to write His apocalypse, He mentions the earth's rulers as kings all the way up to Revelation 21:24. There will be no elections in eternity, and according to scripture and revelations of its authorities, every position is appointed. Those who would campaign for eternal positions, so to speak, are doing so now. The best model to show us how God's realm installs leaders is found in scripture under all the Lord's references to the words, "He that endures to the end," and the numerous times the words appoint, chose, ordain, and elect appear in scripture in relation to divine service.

Collectively, they appear well over two hundred times. When one leaves this world, whatever his or her spiritual condition and station is determines what that person does forever. Here is what scripture means when it declares that our works follow us. The elect means something entirely different to God than it does to us. To the Lord elect means what He has chosen, foreordained based on His own decisions. For humans the election campaign happens in the here and now. When we all rise from the dead, God's inauguration takes place. At that time, all voting will be closed and tallied; the one to make the final decision is the Man whom God has "ordained to be Judge of the quick and the dead," Acts 10:42.

The Ecclesia

Any discussion of the church's ministries and ministers would be wanting without some attention given to the reason it and they exist. As said earlier, the *ecclesia* is meant to establish the Lord Jesus' body as a literal mirror of His world in the one. That reflection is best identified as a satellite. By design, satellites are meant to be obsequious, that is compliant, obedient, and submissive. They are created to yield completely to the will of another, the maker or master as a devoted servant. The earth then was made to be heaven's satellite, the church in particular satellites the Lord Jesus' kingdom. The church, as the Lord's manifest kingdom satellite is to accomplish specific tasks and perform definite actions for Him and on His behalf. The Ecclesia as God's Kingdom Satellite is to serve the same or a very similar purpose as a fabricated satellite; it is just not made by hands. In political contexts, a satellite is a country (in our case a world) dependent upon a more powerful one. It refers to a colony, territory, and settlement. In addition, a satellite is synonymic with the word cohort that includes in its many meanings, accomplice, aide, ally, disciple, and attendant. Collateral is another synonym for the world satellite, as is accessory, subordinate, and province. From all these words, it is easy to see that the church as Jesus Christ envisioned it was destined to be more than a weekly gathering site for periodic refreshing, or even an inspired mercy distribution center. Additional terms for this interestingly applied word to the church include the following.

A Satellite Is

1. An attendant
2. A client state
3. A prince's attaché
4. A powerful person, object, or influence
5. A revolutionary planet
6. An accompaniment
7. Equipment or appliances that orbit another
8. The earth's or the moon's orbiter
9. A person who follows or serves another
10. An orbiting celestial body
11. A broadcaster
12. A disseminator

What does this say about the church and its destiny from the mind of the Lord? For all these reasons, the New Creation church or as the Savior called in scripture, His ecclesia was born is sustained by eternity. Upon recognition of Jesus as the promised Messiah, the Lord told Peter that He would give Him the keys of the kingdom of heaven and whatever he (Peter) bound on earth would be bound in heaven and what Peter loosed on earth would be loosed in heaven. His statement unfolds the satellite connection between the heavens and the earth, also why it is indispensable to the Creator. The meanings of the word satellite shed some light on the Lord's enigmatic declaration and explain the earth's inexplicable tie to the heavens whether it understands it or not.

The Lord bestowed upon Peter this amazing honor as He revealed His eternal ecclesia, the one His Father held in store for His Son. Ecclesia is the Greek word for the Savior's eternal New Creation institution. It is called the *ecclesia* because it, like the word's meaning, is God's body of "called out ones." Christ's ecclesia like everything that He returned to His and His Father's dominion, existed before time began. See Ephesians 1:4; 1 Corinthians 2:7; 2 Timothy 1:9; and Titus 1:2. What Jesus called back into His kingdom's eternal realms did indeed have an earthly counterpart. Its existence at the time Jesus gave

Peter heaven's kingdom keys helped the apostle know what the Messiah handed over to him, as did the others. That institution having its origins in ancient Athens was still functioning during Jesus' earthly ministry. To God, the ecclesia was more than a religious gathering; it was a literal governing institution that determined, decreed, deliberated, and legislated the sacred and secular. Some of its functions and authorities in Greek times were:

- Legislation

- Military decrees

- Finance

- Convening and conducting public court

- Criminal investigations

- Deciding and meting out penalties

- Judicial functions and decisions

- Public works

- Official elections

- War and peace declarations

- Ostracism

In addition to these was handling and deciding with the senate matters of state of supreme importance were concerning:

- War

- Peace

- Treaties

- Alliances

- Military regulations

- Accept or reject proposals from various other councils and authorities

    a. Finance and economy

    b. Import and exports

    c. New religions

    d. Rites, observances, celebrations and festivals

    e. Commendations and honors

f.   Conferring citizenship

From this list, it is easy to see what Jesus Christ thought of His eternal assembly of "called out ones" in relation to His pervasive rule of all creation. It explains His words to the eleven in John 20:23: *"Whose soever sins ye remit, they are remitted unto them; and whose soever sins ye retain, they are retained."*

Confirming Ecclesiastical Citizenship

Regarding the Graeco-Roman Ecclesia's membership, naturalized citizenship was mandatory. Considering the empire's vast conquest of other nations, the wisdom of the requirement and its political expediency are obvious. To assure only genuine members entered ecclesiastical gatherings and participated in its officiations, a six-member governing board of the Ecclesia verified the right of a person to attend its meetings. This board, once called the *lexiarchi*, registered everyone that became citizens of the state. When session was called, every entrant's record was checked against the registry of all those approaching the hall to participate in the meetings. Whoever was not registered as a naturalized citizen was prevented from entering the ecclesia's gathering hall. Here is the premise of Paul's discussion with the chief captain that arrested him without first ascertaining status as a Roman citizen. Both types of citizenship are mentioned in Acts 22:27-29; Paul was a natural born citizen and the captain purchased his. How much does this mirror the work of the five-fold in its required authentication of those born again by the Holy Spirit?

The Lord Jesus upholds heaven's policy of confirming a Christian's legitimate citizenship as redemption: born again, born from above, filled with His Spirit, and sealed by the Holy Ghost. Those approaching His kingdom and attempting to gain entrance into its proceedings or access to its privileges must pass under the all-seeing surveillance eye of the eternal God. The modern idea that all are entitled to the New Creation Ecclesia's blessings, privileges, and authority is false.   Since time began, governments have always reserved their best benefits for legitimate citizens. Their constitutions exist to see to it. The King of glory, according to His Father's scriptures, does the same. His famous words in John chapter 10:7-9 declare it: *"Then said Jesus unto them again, Verily, verily, I say unto you, I am the door of the sheep. All that ever came before me are thieves and robbers: but the sheep did not hear them. I am the door: by me if any man enter in, he shall be saved, and shall go in and out, and find pasture."*

Although His words leave room for the reality of interlopers creeping in pretending to be saved for the right to enter His fold, His door metaphor nonetheless suggests that He is not lenient in the matter. God is not oblivious to imposters that feign redemption and Christ's parable of Matthew 13:47-51 underscores this eternal truth. It is true that Jesus is the door to His flock, but that meant more to Him than it seems to mean today. Doors, many modernists like to forget, swing both ways. They open and shut, as the Savior says in Revelation chapter three. Doors open to allow access and close to prevent it. If the Lord wanted to give the impression that His was a one-way revolving door, His language would have reflected it.

As the Shepherd of God's flock, Jesus is the keeper of its gates. He knows what qualifies souls to access heaven's blessings (Ephesians 1:3 calls them spiritual blessings in heavenly places). Later in Ephesians 3:12 the Lord stipulates how a human may legally access and enjoy heaven's treasures. Not only does the Lord comprehend heaven's criteria for admitting and responding to a mortal, His spiritual staff knows as well who should or should not avail themselves of His provisions. That is the purpose of this discussion. Paul's words in 2 Timothy 2:19 makes the point best of all: *"Nevertheless the foundation of God standeth sure, having this seal, The Lord knoweth them that are his. And, Let every one that nameth the name of Christ depart from iniquity."* That wisdom underlay the Lord's revelation of His church and His teaching on Himself as its true shepherd.

In the ancient ecclesiastical model, non-citizens had no right to enter ecclesiastical conventions and were subject to bodily eviction if they sneaked in without the necessary approval or credentials. Considering the size of its assembly, being called to this duty required diligence, vigilance, and dedication to the pure integrity of its proceedings. The officer assigned to see to the purity of the gathering was called "sergeant at arms." According to the *Dictionary of Classical Mythology, Religion, Literature, and Art*, there was also someone over the ecclesia called a president and a higher institution over it called a *Boule* or *Bule* or *Curia* (the word used for royal court). The pattern broadens typical explanations of Peter's initiation to Christ's apostleship.

CHAPTER FIVE

The Five-Fold Offices

Chapter Topics:

The Five-Fold: Ancient Concepts Serve New Testament Function • Discovering and Applying This Teaching • Association Method of Teaching • The Bible's Premise: Eternity in the Now • Jesus' Doctrine from Heaven • Our Best Sin's Rest • Compensatory Accommodations • Human Brilliance Compensates for Sin Condition • Archaic Struggles with Sin's Grip • Human Worship from Adam to Christ

---

This chapter elaborates further on what has become known as the five-fold offices of the Church of the Lord Jesus Christ to take you from God's heart to His Church's ministry, and then to the kingdom's ministry world. The ways used to analyze and compare the language chosen by God in Scripture for the offices and their functions come from their natural or earthly counterparts. They are taken from biblical and secular positions you are no doubt familiar with in life, whose functions equate to what an officer does in the world. Comparing the E-4 officers with agents in any other organization establishes their labors and authority as the work Christian ministers are to do for Christ as officers of His church.

In keeping with Jesus' model of making the heavenly and eternal plain to the flesh, we resort to accepted professional attitudes toward agents in any organization to make our point. People immediately envision what an insurance, political or government agent's role and authority is in their fields. They are accustomed to encountering and even voting in agents in clubs, fraternities, sororities, and other social groups. Few need explanation of what the title means to their world. This is not so with the church. The church's officials are not official, their agents do not represent their sender or founder, and authority is delegated from the head up and not from heaven down. For these reasons, great confusion surrounds God's vision, use, and endorsement of Paul's Ephesians 4:11 ministers. Rarely are they linked to his 1 Corinthians 12:28, 29 ordinations.

The Five-Fold: Ancient Concepts Serve New Testament Function

The concept of God's Divine Order presented in Ephesians 4:11 is not new. It is not strictly a New Testament Institution. The idea of a conglomerate entity springing from a central core (the church) branching out into distinct functions is dated. The Old Testament period alludes to a similar institution comprising a body of class ministers sent to perform the specialized activities of a federalized purpose. The substance of their institution resembles, broadly, the New Testament church institution described by the Apostle Paul as a single ministry corporation. It is the Old Testament shadow known as the *Melakim*. Its noun is *Malak* and defines a messenger representative. The term's meaning includes the tasks carried out by one who is a representative. These tasks can be as simple as carrying a single message or as complex as executing a special commission. Whichever it is, the term stresses that the messenger represents his or her sender.

For the duration of the assignment, the functionary and the sender are expeditiously one and the same. Those who serve this institution must above all have a message, as message bearing is central to the necessity of any communications service. This requirement applies whether the assignment is a commission, a mission, a task, duty, function, or errand. Melakim officers can be judges, guardians, deliverers, or protectors of God's property, His glory, possessions, and premises. Their status could be royal, judicial, military, priestly, civil, custodial, and even clerical (administrative). Whatever the level or classification they initially represent as a corporate body, God's ministers are never relieved of expressing His presence and glory. It gives them their distinctive from their secular counterparts. The mentality of such a servant was that they cease to be as individual and became, while in His service, the mind, will, wisdom, and sentiments of God. Definitively, the *Melakim* could be an intercessor or a herald, a teacher, a prophet, or a priest. From this, the mysterious institution that foreshadowed the church Paul was charged with organizing and establishing is discerned. Its structure and staff were unquestionably well known to Paul, a former Sanhedrist. Surely, his previous career's knowledge influenced his concept of the New Creation church as designed by the Lord's Church.

The *Melakim's* duties, depending upon the position, involved messaging to include announcing, summoning, declaring and informing beyond simple postal delivery. These activities easily reflect the roles of the evangelist and the teacher in the church. In this capacity prophecy, diplomacy, espionage, behavior restraint, and ingathering all surface as integral to this generic body. Also, among them could be found the duties of guardianship that characterize the pastor, the prophet, and the apostle. In the ministry spectrum, priestly functions, the highest of God's callings, stand out most that the New Testament church accepts are the entire responsibility of the church of Jesus Christ according to 1 Peter 2:19. Not only did this institution officiate over the "*religio*-spiritual" matters of God's possession, but they were stewards of the nation's temporal affairs as well. These were business people, craftsmen, goods merchandiser's, skilled laborers, ministers, and professionals. You could find them performing routine tasks and projects related to the mission of spreading God's message, and as professional bureaucrats officiating the kingdom's governmental affairs. These servants were, unquestionably, God-endowed for their work, regardless of its nature, and were rendered productive by an unending supply of His Spirit.

No other institution researched could better mirror the 1 Corinthians 12:28, 29 and Ephesians 4:11 Church. No term better describes its proposed function from God's mind. The titles may differ, somewhat—scribes, sages, seers, and rabbis—instead of those employed by Paul for the Church; nevertheless, the concept and its express labors are clearly recognized in this Old Testament shadow. Even the ministry of helps is provided for in its explanation. The professional, the royal, the bureaucrat, the craftsman and merchant, the skilled laborer and the producer all fit within the framework of the *Melakim*. Moreover, its objective is similar to the Church as attained through the union and assignments of the Lord Jesus. Matthew 28:18-20 and Mark 16:15-20 plainly show the divinely approved work shifted, as with all the Old Testament custodies, from the natural to the spiritual; from the localized to the universal. Now the Church composed of all nations, peoples, and tongues sees to the generation after generation business of proclaiming God, discipling His offspring, shepherding His flock, and declaring His present truth. They attend to

His affairs and regain control of His Creation from the hands and rule of darkness.

Discovering and Applying This Teaching

Several factors were considered in researching this material: purpose and function, conditions and climate, environment and consciousness, in addition to humanity's state of existence in relation to God's goal for it. The approach used to present this teaching is consistent with that used by the Lord Jesus when He taught those who followed His earthly ministry. Christ exercised His ministry by staying with the premise His Father God used throughout the record of His dealings with humanity. He based His teachings on much of what the people already understood and practiced to establish His new kingdom.

One clear way to understand the Lord's approach is to go back and draw on God's historical dealings with people and the earth. From the moment of Adam's fall, the Lord's means and methods of contacting and interacting the man and His wife had to change. Where formerly their Creator was first and only, another element entered the mentality of His creaturehood, making God resort to naturalistic means of revealing Himself to His creation. Instead of being inclined toward God as their Creator, humanity now wrestled with a dark hostile force that stood in the way. This new force literally barricaded God's path to man, and man's path to his God. Since God and His ways were now alien to Adam, the Lord retreated to rely on heavenly intermediaries, mostly His angels. This ushered in the first of humanity's new eras. Under Adam's new era, people stumbled through sin's darkness to learn what was once apparent. Consequently, he needed other ways to access his Maker to practice his religion, relearn some form of worship, and grasp God's righteousness.

Seeing the long term effects of Adam's decision, God now let the darkness precede the light and allow sin to be the ground for human schooling and righteousness. Unavoidably, the Lord's new method of interacting with man was to let them get it whatever they learned wrongly so long as they got it. You see righteousness ceased to be people's start point for any initiative. Darkness took over and all that humans attempted sprang from it, leaving God's initial approach to restoring His light in humankind to be that of ignorance instead of wisdom, death and not life, wrong and not right. This pattern is seen in everything. People have to be taught to do what they want. They have to learn how not to fail, lie, err or destroy. These are all features of Adam's satanic inheritance and the God of all creation permitted it. Later, He could reverse it by returning truth and the light to the planet and the world to make it right. Based on these facts, the Lord's primary means of educating His creation became that of association;

71

that is, using a familiar thing to instruct them about another. Jesus' use of parables foretold by the Psalmist in 78:1-3 conforms to the method; thus, the reason for the phrase *Association Method of Teaching* discussed below.

Association Method of Teaching

To teach them His ways, an alternative means of divine instruction was required. God chose what we call here the Association Method of teaching predicated upon Psalm 111:10 and Proverbs 9:10. The Association Method means He draws on the accumulation of facts, customs, history, behaviors, and beliefs people already embrace. He uses their language (slang included), their loves, and passions—and yes, even their idols—to shatter their myths, uproot superstitions, and redirect their focus to Creator God. Christ, in whom is hid all the treasures of wisdom and knowledge (Colossians 2:3), taught parables using the people's major commerce, agriculture. He used employment, military, and domestic practices to call their attention to the elements of divine truth hidden in their lifestyles. He used entertainment, amusements, and anything else they related to in the world to unlock humanity's darkness and prepare them for God's kingdom light.

From ancient times eternity has weaved its wisdom and truth throughout human history. Psalm 49:1-4 says as much:

> *"To the chief Musician, A Psalm for the sons of Korah. Hear this, all ye people; give ear, all ye inhabitants of the world: Both low and high, rich and poor, together. My mouth shall speak of wisdom; and the meditation of my heart shall be of understanding. I will incline mine ear to a parable: I will open my dark saying upon the harp."*

The Bible's Premise: Eternity in the Now

All that the Lord does and is doing comes from His eternal front and not our ancient foundations. More that ten times the phrase *"foundation of the world"* is used to describe Christ's approach to presenting Israel's God as the source of His enduring truth. The Bible is its consummate statement of God's success since time began.

1. *That it might be fulfilled which was spoken by the prophet, saying, I will open my mouth in parables; I will utter things which have been kept secret from the foundation of the world. Matthew 13:35 KJV*

2. *Then shall the King say unto them on his right hand, Come, ye blessed of my Father, inherit the kingdom prepared for you from the foundation of the world. Matthew 25:34 KJV*

3. *That the blood of all the prophets, which was shed from the foundation of the world, may be required of this generation. Luke 11:50 KJV*

4. *Father, I will that they also, whom thou hast given me, be with me where I am; that they may behold my glory, which thou hast given me: for thou lovedst me before the foundation of the world. John 17:24 KJV*

5. *According as he hath chosen us in him before the foundation of the world, that we should be holy and without blame before him in love. Ephesians 1:4 KJV*

6. *For we which have believed do enter into rest, as he said, As I have sworn in my wrath, if they shall enter into my rest: although the works were finished from the foundation of the world. Hebrews 4:3 KJV*

7. *For then must he often have suffered since the foundation of the world: but now once in the end of the world hath he appeared to put away sin by the sacrifice of himself. Hebrews 9:26 KJV*

8. *Who verily was foreordained before the foundation of the world, but was manifest in these last times for you. 1 Peter 1:20 KJV*

9. *And all that dwell upon the earth shall worship him, whose names are not written in the book of life of the Lamb slain from the foundation of the world. Revelation 13:8 KJV*

10. *The beast that thou sawest was, and is not; and shall ascend out of the bottomless pit, and go into perdition: and they that dwell on the earth shall wonder, whose names were not written in the book of life from the foundation of the world, when they behold the beast that was, and is not, and yet is. Revelation 17:8 KJV*

Three times the New Testament comments on what eternity was doing "before the foundation of the world."

1. *Father, I will that they also, whom thou hast given me, be with me where I am; that they may behold my glory, which thou hast given me: for thou lovedst me before the foundation of the world. John 17:24 KJV*

2. *According as he hath chosen us in him before the foundation of the world, that we should be holy and without blame before him in love: Ephesians 1:4 KJV*

3. *Who verily was foreordained before the foundation of the world, but was manifest in these last times for you. 1 Peter 1:20 KJV*

To the above, we may add:

4. *And now, O Father, glorify thou me with thine own self with the glory which I had with thee before the world was. John 17:5 KJV*

5. *But we speak the wisdom of God in a mystery, even the hidden wisdom, which God ordained before the world unto our glory 1 Corinthians 2:7 KJV :*

6. *Who hath saved us, and called us with an holy calling, not according to our works, but according to his own purpose and grace, which was given us in Christ Jesus before the world began. 2 Timothy 1:9 KJV*

7. *In hope of eternal life, which God, that cannot lie, promised before the world began. Titus 1:2 KJV*

As you can see, our Savior did not make up His doctrine or distill His own wisdom as He went along. He stayed with what He and His Father had been saying and doing since before time began, referring to John 17:5, 2 Timothy 1:9, and Titus 1:2.

Jesus' Doctrine from Heaven

When teaching on the subject of heaven, Jesus employed an earthly replica or similitude, because His audience could readily grasp the visible and earthly. Eleven times He begins a parable with "the kingdom of heaven is like;" all of them are in Matthew's gospel. For a portrait of what He presented as the kingdom of heaven, as distinguished from the kingdom of God, look at His analogies. The kingdom of heaven is like:

1. A seed sower

2. A mustard seed

3. Leaven hidden in three measures of meal (three reflecting

4. the Godhead)

5. Hidden treasure in a field

6. An ambitious merchant's pearl (wisdom) of great price

7. A dragnet of mixed fish

8. A well learnt householder's (landlord's) old and new

9. treasures

10. A king settling his accounts

11. A landlord hiring vineyard workers

12. A king arranging his son's marriage

13. An ordained king entrusting his favored servants with his kingdom while we went off to war to inherit it.

The last one parallels Luke 19:11-27, Jesus' parable of the ten pound or mina that is often confused with the parable of the ten talents.

When explaining the nature of His kingdom and installing His first officers, the Lord chose names and titles reasonably familiar to His followers so they would easily understand what He transferred to God's eternal kingdom. That understanding they would later draw from as patterns to administrate what the Son of Man entrusted to them. Psalm 29:9-14 tell why.

The basis for the Lord's teaching method, as you can see from the Scripture references, stemmed from the natural darkness, ignorance, and opposition to God humanity is born with because of the law of sin and death Adam passed on through his seed. While we all know the story, time and events have shown not everyone is aware of its effects and new generations have to be told as their elders either remind them, after they have been reminded of it themselves, if need be.

Our Best Sin's Rest

Throughout the centuries, the story of man's fall and doom has been ridiculed, romanced, distorted, downplayed, and even rewritten. What happened in Eden continues to unfold the plot with its spiritual and natural consequences, and physical side effects shaping every area of life. Those blinded by its stronghold minimize sin's apparent sovereignty by treating it much the same way as the guilty overlook or play down their faults and missteps. To soften its sting and humiliation, sin as God calls it is normalized as no big deal, a counteractive tactic to cause sufferers to shift its cause to the solution. Over time, the strategy, successfully severing cause from effect, exalted humanist remedies over God's truth.

Christ's ministers, though, are duty bound not to buy into the tactic. Skillfully refusing not to beat down their audiences with the truth, they have an obligation to limit their delusions nonetheless. The

Ephesians 4:11 ministers must always motivate people to want God, to see Him as worth it all and not allow them to settle for the world's corruptions, deceptions, and destruction. They should know that their best does not even amount to God's least "because the foolishness of God is wiser than men and His weakness is stronger than men," 1 Corinthians 1:25. Mortals must know how and why the verse before this one declares Christ alone as God's power and wisdom.

Loyalty to the call to Christian ministry requires God's servants to keep all His truths and counsel before people so that they do not think the best of this life is better than the Creator's afterlife. God wants humanity to know that His eternal life holds the answers to this life's disappointments and suffering; that He truly made man upright as Solomon states in Ecclesiastes 7:29, *"but they have sought out many inventions."* If the church's New Testament ministry officers fail in their duty, people fear death, want to cling to this pitiable world, and worse yet, renounce and reject the Creator's perfect sacrifice in favor of everlasting damnation. Promoting the upside of God's grace as if the world itself were redeemed from its curse by downplaying the reason God condemned it in the first place, is a dangerous proposition that is sheer fantasy. On its own, it is tantamount to hallucination and shows such ministers are ill equipped to grasp God's view of humanity's fundamental condition or that they reject for the world's lie. That is, that all have sinned and come short of the Maker's glory.

Human inventions (Solomon's word), no matter how superior to preceding generations, remain inferior to God. Though they are vital to earthly life, they are still no more than compensations for the human deficiencies and frailties that arose out of, and continue to emerge from, Adam's transgression. They are certainly not God's best for His creaturehood. The very needs themselves confirm the Lord's reason for the Church (Christ's body of called-out ones) and its ministries, powerful dispensation and operations, and His officers. Technology, science, and medicine, in this text, are called Compensatory Accommodations to explain their motivation of meeting humankind's *"sindom"* needs. The phrase is to emphasize their sole purpose of compensating for the mortal shortfalls common to man that rob people of the Creator's best in life.

Compensatory Accommodations

Religious tradition has made it not only unpopular to recall the sin the human race plunged into, but also risky to do so as well. Prevalent church teachings push the upswing outcome of the cross severing it from the downside of the fall that necessitated it. Both must be *equally understood* if the God's institutions are to be regarded and the

compensatory accommodations that rival it are to be rightly addressed.

By **compensatory accommodations**, we mean the adjustments, designs, inventions, and implementations God, and men through Him, employ to overcome and offset sin's ravages. Though they are essential to man, they often obstruct the Lord's hand and hinder His will and redemption in the process because they lulled the flesh into thinking it can fix itself. In reality, they merely ease the burden of God's curse. If you were to think about all this carefully, you would acknowledge that much of what we praise as human advancement and technological explosion just compensate for the shortfalls sin kneaded into human nature. Should the Bible be taken honestly again, this truth would become evident to the astute thinker and the reasonable scholar.

Here are a few cases that substantiate our premise that the majority of human inventions are required to relieve the hardship of human life destroyed by sin. For instance, consider the motivation behind those discussed below. Many ministers have been reared in a completely humanist environment where man is the center of God's universe and sin is merely an impersonal enemy that prevents or perverts life for those on earth. They have no idea of how exceedingly sinful sin really is.

The disorders, dysfunctions, and frailties that technology so wonderfully remedies are no more than proof of sin's devastation at work in people. Mortality is a curse of death and the obligation to transform all human negatives into positives, to deny or cover them, all verify the Lord's word is true. People die physically because they are born dead spiritually, which is also why they age. The flesh decays and decomposes because the human spirit, however mutated to earth it may be, is devoid of its Creator's life. It is compelled to return to the dust when its portion of natural life ruptures or is expended.

Human Brilliance Compensates for Sin Condition

Here are some examples:

Electricity	To remove the darkness that fell on men and the earth that brought his functional life to a grinding halt. Pentecost's arrival of the Holy Spirit, candle light was first invented and later in the 19th century, the light bulb.
Refrigeration	To prolong the life of food from the natural spoilage built into it from the earth's decay, cooling was invented. This

reduced man's physical sickness from his food.

Automation

To speed up the pace of human existence; to facilitate man's travel from one place to another so he could produce, energy restored to the planet by the Holy Spirit allowed motility to replace pedestrianism.

Communication

To enable conversation in distant lands and reconnect the planet shattered by sin's disunity, various means of transmitting sound and sight were invented. What makes this significant is that the Creator has been communicating from afar since before time. Dreams and visions, voices in one's sleep or hearing non-audible sounds are all commonplace technology for the natural world.

Medicine

To reverse, overturn, and stem the tide of physical suffering and maladies caused by the innate corruptions and deteriorations natural to the flesh, different treatments were devised to remedy sickness, disease, age, and catastrophes.

Science

To overall enrich and improve or find the answers for the quality (and improved state of) human life, knowledge (from *gnosis*, another word for science) was developed. It allowed discovery of the mysteries of this and how to modify it to heal, inform, empower, and overall benefit instead of devastate humanity.

Such information was once known and understood by Adam but became locked away from his inherent human intelligence. Science perverted is where humanity strives to overturn his hopelessness apart from his Maker.

Cosmetics

To cover up, modify, and beautify what

sin has marred, distorted or disfigured, an assortment of natural materials were processed to improve appearance, hygiene, or correct severe or mild deformities.

Perfume
This invention compensates for the natural human secretions that offend the senses and are harmful to the body without regular hygiene.

Alcohol
Another word for it may be antidote; alcohol strengthens or numbs the pain and weakness suffered by the embattled and embittered human soul, its broken emotions and ruptured psyche.

Amusement
Not inherently wrong or vain, amusements are manufactured means of momentarily escaping life's harshness by diverting the attention from the vulnerability and temporality of human life.

These are but a few of the human inventions that are necessary because of the law of sin and death at work in humanity. For sure, you can add more to this list yourself but you get the point. Take a little excursion into God's world and the answer to humanism versus eternal life becomes clear. For example, think about insurance, medicine, the media and the host of carnal activities that are normal for us on earth. Some of them are fun, others are essential, but ultimately they are all temporal. Bodies that heal themselves do not need medicine or insurance. People with knowledge and understanding beyond ours will not need as many mistakes nor have accidents.

Aging is a product of the curse. In a place where death no longer exists, insurance is useless. The same is true with medicine in a place where the trees renew their leaves monthly to heal the nations without cost. While we are on the subject, the question arises, "What about the media?" The answer varies little from our theme, what the darkened mind alienated from its Maker's life enjoys as entertainment is utterly despised in a place where righteous and holiness reign. All these contrivances compensate for the sin born in humans. When the law of sin and death are removed, what sustains and enriches the lives of eternal beings is drastically different.

Over fifty percent of what this life has to offer in business, industry, education, science, and technology subsists on the very effective coup Satan pulled off in the Garden of Eden. As a result, the faculties, capacities, mentality, and physique God intended humankind to enjoy in His world became flawed. Instead of the Heavenly Age, once mankind fell in Adam's seed everyone was left to drudge through the Sin Age until Jesus' millennial reign and ultimately God's new world under His everlasting reign. Roman 5:12-14 clearly makes this point. Until that time, discovery after discovery helped humanity advance from the Stone Age to the present, just to reach the place where we are today, surviving as a race, recapturing at every stage some semblance of Adam's former glory. Sadly, the height of human advancements is no more than a means to ease the burden of his life and elevate man above the animals.

Archaic Struggles with Sin's Grip

Meanwhile, during humanity's arduous drudge through its dark pedestrian age, from primitivism to now, God was in the background helping nudging and preserving its seed as best He could. People's spiritual light, completely extinguished by Adam's fall severed, thus alienated them from their Maker. To restore them, God instituted a series of religious programs to redirect people's worship back to Him and in due course, exchange natural religions and their rituals for eternal redemption and restored oneness with Him. These, the Lord did in the midst of the carnal strongholds and demonic imaginations Cain's posterity inflicted and still inflicts on His world. Inescapable darkness within, and without, motivate people's attempts to recover God's best without His help.

Human Worship from Adam to Christ

Failed approaches to worship began with Adam after his surrender in Eden, known as his fall. They extended through the flood until they culminated in the fulfillment of God's dream in His Son Jesus Christ. Then the passages of scriptures like John 5:22-30--judgment, Ephesians 2:1,2--death; 1 Corinthians 15:20-22—death in Adam— ceased to be true for the redeemed. Humanity ceased to be alienated from God, dead in trespasses and sins, and dead in Adam because of sin. Instead, the human race was reunited in Christ. The cross forgave and saved by God's grace so those believing in Jesus Christ were made alive—quickened by the Son of God's love. At least one third of man's being is immediately revived by the redemptive work of Christ's cross. What are left to preserve are the other two thirds. Progressively, these are restored, repaired, and revived until death, the last enemy, is destroyed and the whole can be regenerated.

By now, you realize that God planned *all* this is to be accomplished through His Church *(See Ephesians chapters 1 & 2)*. For it to do so, since He was closing out His government's Mosaic age, the Lord brought forward an encoded prophecy from Psalm 68:18. Here is a notable portion of it. *"You have ascended on high; you have led captivity captive; you have received gifts among men, even among the rebellious, that the Lord God might dwell there."* It resurfaces in Paul's letter to the Ephesians, 4:8. *"Wherefore he saith, When he ascended up on high, he led captivity captive, and gave gifts unto men."* Wisdom that God's ministers must posses and His ecclesiastical officials must uphold, it conforms minister sermonizing to His judgment on the world: that all have sinned and come short of His glory. With unprecedented implications for Creator and creature, the passage immutably answers the devilish doctrines spawned by Satan's seducing spirits that convince people they are better than their Maker. God's Son has led captivity captive and thereby overthrown the devious philosophies and rhetoric inspired by ancient supernatural masterminds (1 Corinthians 2:6-8).

Today they only push their pagan and occultic genre over today's airways because the typical Christian allows it, intentionally or not. Jude's fallen spirits and Paul's spiritual hosts empower the people responsible for their obscene, incestuous, adulterous and pornographic swill to saturate the modern consciousness; selling their platform that humans are in charge of their own destiny and so are capable of their own soul's salvation. From casual circles to revered universities, the falsehood is promoted as sophistication to which only the secular can mind conform. Infecting community, law and government, politics and professionals, the message is the same. God is taboo, Judeo-Christian religion is the enemy, and the Holy Bible must be removed as a demonic barrier. Boldly or subtly, it is touted and peddled worldwide to race the cosmos to its appointed end. Deadly spiritual forces driven by a vile eternal agenda relentlessly goad lost souls and minds into imagining and pursuing their dark depravity. They push upon us the macabre; the gristly imbed their psyche with a savage desire to decriminalize their destruction.

CHAPTER SIX

Christ's Ministry Answers It All

Chapter Topics:

Gifts unto Men: The Kind of Gifts Christ Gave • The Gift is an
Officer • The Meaning of an Officer • The Weight of an Office • 46
Five-Fold Duties • The 15 Standard Features of an Office • Validity
of Explanation • Describing an Office •The Entrustment of an Office
• Why Offices Persist

Decoded in Ephesians, written approximately A.D. 60-61,
verse 4:11 shows Paul's revelation of the Church's
leadership and hierarchy. Linking Psalms 68:18 with
Ephesians 4:11, the apostle named the fundamental offices
of the Church and defined their purposes. To lay the
foundation for his revelation Paul draws the Old Testament
prophecy forward and sets it in the heart of his New Testament
unveiling.

Reminding us of Christ's finished work, he reiterates that Jesus
ascended on high, led captivity captive, and gave gifts to men.
Immediately, Paul answers any rising questions over the ascension.
Christ who descended, he asserts, has now ascended. Paul's purpose
was to show how Jesus fulfilled and fills all things. After returning
home, Jesus Christ distributed those Psalms 68 gifts within the Church
because He completed what it took Him to inherit those gifts of

82

human treasures, the souls of those that believed Him to deposit within them heavenly gifts and talents. Now Jesus is able to give them to His Church to establish (found, build up, and stabilize) it. These human gifts, perpetually staff, manage, cover, care for, and nurture God's holy habitation in the flesh *throughout* its earthly existence. What follows next is a discussion of those Psalm 68 gifts and their officiality in God's kingdom.

Gifts unto Men: The Kind of Gifts Christ Gave

The word for gifts as used in Ephesians 4:8 is the Greek word, *Doma* from the Greek term *Didomi* (Psalm 68:18). The first word means, "A gift; a present," connoting the <u>presentation</u> of a gift. The second term qualifies what was presented. In our instance, the gift was a "bestowal." Regarding Paul's subject, the gifts are the bestowal of a ministry in all its accompanying powers is meant. The implication is that the gifts were the E-4 officers set in the Church for eternal purposes that integrate the fullness of *Didomi's* meaning as brought forth from God. These officers committed themselves (and were committed), granted and were granted, received, showed or demonstrated what the Godhead would do in its stead. God set the E-4 offices in place to do throughout the world through Christ's Church only what those redeemed from the law of sin and death could accomplish on His level. They show the world the Godhead at work in human vessels, what 2 Corinthians 4:7 intends. Christ's gifts assure His wisdom, treasures, righteousness, favor, grace, operations, manifestations, demonstrations and revelations are dispensed in the world until its end. Minimally, these nine dispensations enable the five-fold, and the church at large, for what God needs done in their generations.

Although the offices were gifts, *bestowals and presentations,* their authority and esteem were not diminished or slighted. The gift aspect came into play when the Psalmist added, almost as a postscript, *"Even the rebellious, that the Lord God might dwell there."* The rebellious in question were, of course, the converts who were once Satan's property, former vessels of his habitation. Going beyond the literal children of Abraham, the Almighty extended His grace to a chosen number of Gentiles from the world. They are the rebellious the Lord meant back in the Psalms.

Now that Christ had finished His Calvary work, the rebellious heathens or nations, became Jesus' prize trophies (John 17:2) as part of the New Creation vessels He redeemed for the Godhead's holy habitation. Subsequently, these souls snatched out of the world for Christ, were *given* portions of His remaining mission and ministry. Through them, Jesus oversees and tends His flock. Also, through them

He continues evangelizing, prophesying, and teaching from His heavenly throne manifested in the officials He ordained to keep His Church going. Hence, the gift application explains the meaning of Ephesians 2:8-10. Collectively these constituted what came to be known as the five-fold offices of the church.

As a new organization, the church's staff members were endowed supernaturally from the start. All they received was given to them freely by God *(see Matthew 10)*. No one went to school to qualify the Lord's posts, at least not formally, although more than fifteen thousand hours of direct instruction from God's Son more than qualified the twelve apostles for their ministries. That amounts to more than three hundred and twenty-five credit hours—more than eighty hours more than a doctorate. This alone established them as approved by God instead of man. Since it was outside the structure of traditional Jewish education, not one of them bought or otherwise earned their ministries. Christ's apostles were, as John chapter six and fifteen maintains, chosen beforehand by Christ. Based on their precedence, the Lord established that formal schooling fails (on its own) to "qualify" His ministers for their preordained offices. In addition, nor does it establish one's professional readiness before the Lord. What school does is help the minister to do a better job; it improves the official's skill, wisdom, and overall performance. Whether a person is capable of performing well in the job or not in the beginning does not affect their divine call to Christ's ministry. Ineptitude, inexperience, or lack of knowledge will not annul God's call. If not corrected, they will just in the end discredit the minister and cause the fruit of the ministry to be immature, unripe, or non-existent.

The previous explanation shows the context in which the word "gift" is appropriately applied in scripture. Were you to think about it carefully you would conclude this makes perfect sense in light of who God. You see anything the Lord gives humans falls under the classification of a gift since nothing God's creatures receive from Him can be earned. In no way could a person qualify himself or herself for His ministry. No one could buy their call from Him, possess or ever produce or generate enough to give the Lord in exchange for His predestinies on our lives. What could one trade Him for bestowals with what type of currency? Our corruptible moneys certainly will not do. Therefore, to clarify how we receive from the Lord, He informs us that He gives and we receive. The dispensations God imparts are termed as "gifts" in this context. From here, we address the reference to the *Ephesians' staff* as officers.

The Gift is an Officer

If you are a traditionally developed Christian, the words *church clergy* are quite unfamiliar to you who are accustomed to seeing them as strictly ministers, God's servants, and no more; and this they are. All the same, though, there is much more to be learned about what God had in mind when He decreed His ministry choices and applied His select titles to them. Clearly, He had a bigger picture in mind. What the Lord did not have in mind was minister self-aggrandizement or the inflation of soulish egos. First Thessalonians tells us God did not intend the degradation and abuse of His officers commonly seen today as a preventative against sheep abuse. God's gift to a dark chaotic world is His order. Hence, when God blesses anything, He first grants it the wisdom of His divine order. The essence of His gifts to the church is to know His order and experience its peace.

The way the term *officer* applies in Scripture, the accompanying explanations covey their value simply expressed in one word: **respect**. Our purpose is to show how the popular "equality for all" doctrine ascribed to God's ministers flattened their stations over applying God's "no respecter of people" premise that has proved damaging. The major problem is that what people do not respect, they will not heed. Failure to heed makes Christians prey to Satan and his maneuvers. The tragic result is Hebrews 13:17: the officers' ministries cease to be profitable to those they serve. To address the misnomers, the following information was compiled and presented to correct the misconception. Starting with what the typical dictionary and thesaurus say an officer is, the aim is to expand the traditional Christian's view of the ministry and its officials. Hopefully, it will shift the modern church's view from the carnal democratic model that has frustrated the King's work to date to what the eternal God had in mind and perpetuates when He calls anyone to the Ephesians 4:11 posts.

The Meaning of an Officer

An officer, according to several reliable sources, is the following (on your own time, research each term as used for a deeper understanding):

1. An Agent
2. An Executive
3. An Administrator
4. A Judge
5. A President
6. A Minister

7. A General

8. A Chair

9. A Governor

10. A Guardian

11. A Custodian

12. A Prelate

An officer is also:

13. A Steward

14. An Intermediary

15. A Legate

16. A Vice

17. A Consul

18. A Spokesperson

19. An Operative

20. An Intercessor

21. An Implement

22. A Messenger

Suggestion: Research from all sources what each word means, implies, calls for, and exemplifies.

Within the title definitions listed above, the five E-4 servants fill twenty-two explicit roles. Each one's duties move them in and out of their official roles continually as they execute their respective missions and perform their divine mandates. Both *mission* and *mandate* are the reasons for minister's services to the Lord. The positions carry huge responsibilities and consequences for dereliction. Of all the people the Lord anoints to stand in these offices, only a handful know what their mantles and assignments entail. They assure God's benefit flows to those whom these laborers are sent so they "*make full proof of their ministry.*" The above list establishes the basis for the weightiness of their offices.

The Weight of an Office

As officers, considering the span of responsibilities they carry, the functions of the Ephesians 4:11 positions are immense. Many of them, as they go about doing their work, are so efficient they never give thought to what they tackle effectively in their service from day to day.

For an officer to execute his or her position of trust and authority involves the discharge of specially delegated duties. In relation to Christ's church, an officer *prescribes, authorizes, standardizes, and officiate* religious and communal service, which is what makes it a ministry.[2] As such, the officer's ministry, a post of authority, is empowered by derived[3] authority that duly sanctions an official to handle its specific affairs. Offices make up an organization's branches of special concerns such as its government or institution; a meaningful statement that gives insight into what the Lord had in mind. These all generally fall under the headings of departments. When it comes to the New Testament church, its government is God's, its department is Christ's mission, and its institution is the New Creation ecclesia—His body on earth. Those who handle God's branch offices' execute, preside, direct, and mange the affairs of the multitudinous assembly inhabited by His Holy Spirit.

The three departments of the New Creation Church's divine institutions are *Apostle, Prophet, and Teacher* as stated in I Corinthians 12:28.

46 Five-Fold Duties

Here is the gist of what *standing in an office* entails:

1. Communication	2. Legislation
3. Enactment	4. Ordainment
5. Constitution	6. Lawmaking
7. Deliberation	8. Officiation
9. Performing Rites	10. Anointment
11. Confirmation	12. Imposing Rules
13. Regulations	14. Representation
15. Arbitration	16. Mediation
17. Intervention	18. Negotiation
19. Trial	20. Judgment
21. Government	22. Authority

---

2 *By religious, we mean those services detailed and upheld in Scripture, the Holy Bible canonized by the Lord Jesus Christ.

3 Derived means results from, is a consequent of; ensues; passed on, handed down.

23. Commanding	24. Leadership
25. Mastery	26. Headship
27. Directorate	28. Coordination
29. Management	30. Discipline
31. Administration	32. Dispensation
33. Distribution	34. Appointment
35. Installation	36. Inauguration
37. Enforcement	38. Guarding
39. Canon	40. Education
41. Development	42. Planning
43. Operations	44. Decision making
45. Organization	46. Execution[4]

This is but a sketch of what the respective officers do throughout their tenure in God's service. Some things, are constant, others are intermittent. Some carry over from post to post; others are distinct to the office's title and status and show up with greater frequency and intensity in one officer over another. These unique functions are what make an office an office. They comprise the officiations that constitute it. For the sake of clarification and identification, an analysis, drafted from the meanings and applications of all words above and below, produces a thorough profile of each officer's best attributes that can translate into a job description. Doing so can powerfully enrich the modern Church's understanding of its ministers and their service to God. That is exactly what we suggest you the readers do in the assignment below.

The 15 Standard Features of an Office

[5]Features importantly differentiate one trait or characteristic from others of its kind. They mark what sets one notable quality apart from others. When it comes to an office, the following fifteen qualities typify its representation as part of God's ministry to the church:

    1.   Authority

---

4 <u>Suggestion</u>: Define each term and apply its meanings to what you now understand about the five-fold and God's intent for them.

5 A feature is an essential factor of something that distinguishes its aspects from another.

2. Government

3. Canon

4. Lawmaking

5. Legislation

6. Organization

7. Discipline

8. Teaching

9. Judging

10. Management & Supervision

11. Guardianship

12. Development

13. Officiation of Rites & Sacrament

14. Enforcement

15. Rule

Obviously or not, these fifteen actions will be observed in operation in the ministry of every officer on the planet, as well as in the jurisdiction in which he or she is assigned.

Special Assignment: Students, research first the *forty-six terms* in the manner they appear in the *Meaning of an Officer* and *46 Five-Fold Duties*. Assign each one to a **Ministry Profile** that drafts the officers' work, responsibilities, implied powers, and authority. When completed, share your work with the group next class in a group discussion (as applicable). **Added Suggestion:** Have individual students or group captains present profiles to class before discussion to lay the groundwork for open discussion and critique.

Validity of Explanation

You may be wondering by now what ground there is to attach such broad powers and duties to these positions, and what place have they in they the Lord Jesus Christ's church. The answer to question one is on the ground that of the fifteen features of an office any office that are thus inherited by that officer. If words mean what they say, and definitions convey meaning, context, intent, and usage, with the objective of motivating or altering behavior, then no one who researches the word *officer* (or office for that matter) can argue with its descriptions. Comprehensively, the word **office** contains nineteen elements that feature prominently their fundamental job activities.

The Twenty Elements of an Official's Job Activities

1.	Duty	11.	Rabbi
2.	Function	12.	Mastery
3.	Approach	13.	Standards
4.	Purpose	14.	Principles
5.	Rule	15.	Leadership
6.	Authority	16.	Training
7.	Directive	17.	Nurture
8.	Government	18.	Teaching
9.	Discipline	19.	Legislating
10.	Doctor	20.	Rabbi

Viewing Christ's ministry gifts as *offices*, divine positions of trust spoken, and perceiving how these fundamentals look in God's ministry action, may vivify for you what the Lord expects of His ministers. Spiritually, ecclesiastically, and politically their impact becomes plain. Yes, politics (polis for *polites*) figures prominently in the New Testament ministry. It is the word for citizenship, members of a society, city, or town, and is integral to Christian ministry. Ephesians 2:12 says the church was grafted into Israel's commonwealth. The word translated as commonwealth there is *politeia*, defining a community of citizens. The meaning of a minister as a public servant adds political responsibility and influence to the duties of God's officers. Later discussions of the word *leitourgos* for minister further explain this.

What the E-4 positions themselves define as their duty, function, approach, and purpose further resolve the Lord's intents for installing them. For example, explanations given later for the apostle and prophet, along with their duties, leave no room for doubt regarding their officiates. Investigating the application of the remaining three offices establishes them solidly in the stead of an office. Expanded studies of the word surfaced additional meanings like *rule, authority, directive, government, and discipline* (or *mastery*). When tracing each word's expanded meaning down to its root, we were inevitably brought back to the indispensable attributes of an office. Additionally, the teacher took us to the words *doctor* and *rabbi*. When following this group of definitions, we ended up with discipline, mastery, standards, rule, and principles as their chief features.

With pastors, we also uncovered the words rule, leadership, discipline, training, and nurturing. For the evangelist, exploring this officer led us to the roots of the word *didactic* that imply teaching, legislating and such. No matter how we probed it, the Ephesians 4:11 posts showed up as offices, and that means official. Broadly, the term speaks to authority, governance, power, and headship. The word *post,* a synonym for office in this context, is a synonym for *office.*

From our opening statements on the institutional office of the *Melakim* in Israel, we see that the additional functions of a deputy, an authorized and licensed representative, enter as the root of the God's officiation ordained. Altogether, these terms individually and jointly establish God's Ephesians 4:11 staff as more than gifts in His church. First Corinthians 12:28, 29 upholds this concept and definitely discredits the mere gift application to them.

The above conclusion is further borne out by what Ephesians 4:12-16 reference to the purpose of God's metaphoric hand. It is a straightforward statement of what He expects of the officers. Their ministry functions, roles, and purposes are laid out in this passage. Here is a summary of them:

1. *Perfecting* (*equipping the saints*)—Think about what that calls for.

2. *Work of Ministry*, the object of #1—Consider its demands.

3. E*difying of the body of* Christ—What involvement does this one require?

The Operating Goals of the ministry are:

1. Unity of the faith

2. Knowledge of Jesus Christ

3. Perfect Man

4. Measure and Stature of Christ's Fullness

5. Growth From Spiritual Childhood

6. Wisdom For Doctrinal Stability

7. Discernment of False Doctrine

8. Awareness of Spiritual Manipulation

9. Protection From Spiritual Deceit

10. Avoidance of Deception

11. Instillation of boldly Spoken Truth

12. Balanced Exposition of Truth with Love

13. Growth in All Things

14. Expansion into the Headship of Christ

15. Full Occupation (and preoccupation) of Each Member of the Body with His Mission

16. Equal Distribution and Execution of Christ's Workload

17. Unified Efforts and Labors

18. Uniform Methods and Perspectives

19. Stimulation of the Body's Growth

20. Production of the Body's Self-Edification in Love

Suggestion: Describe practical operations of **1-20** as an assignment.

In studying these operating goals, you will uncover the range of duties, skills, and applications required to accomplish them. These goals can then be broken down into ten achievement categories:

1. Organization
2. Leadership
3. Education
4. Revelation
5. Discipling
6. Attendance and Care
7. Discipline
8. Government
9. Maturation
10. Preparation

Ten simple-sounding steps, but oh, what goes into performing them! Everything involved in planning, orchestrating, implementing, and administrating them to achieve that twenty-point goal list exceeds the traditional view of spiritual, moral, and social ministry. It takes the entire process into the sphere of business and professionalism. Assign one of the operating goals to its relevant category as a developmental exercise. For that, an office—and nothing less than an office—gets the job done. An officer's supreme achievement, because of his or her efforts, is the sanctification of Christ's body from sin to God's truth. The officer's anointing and grace establish it in His righteousness for inheritance and eternal life.

Describing an Office

We have talked much about authority elsewhere in this book. Here we address what Paul and the other New Testament writers understood to be the core, range, and limits of their positions' authority, titles and offices, and what factors and forces make them necessary. You will remember it was said earlier that people do not make the offices, enter but rather it is the office, which **authorizes** the person. Either by precedence or practice, a servant is made an officer because of entering an office. This legally authorizes his or her actions as a principal's representative. By virtue of entering their positions of authority, people are empowered with authority that has most likely resided in the office long before they came along, unless they are the first to occupy it.

An office is the vehicle by which a principal carries out the branch, administration, and operations functions of a mission or commission. Holding an office means exercising the power of the principal that ordained and designed it. It is the responsibility of an office's creator to continually uphold their created offices. The nature an official authority is completely derived from the superior that authored the position, and should be exercised in strict accordance with his or her delegation. An office, once created, subsists on the weight, license, and privileges passed on to each succeeding official occupant. The authorizers of officers must identify and describe the positions' status, accountability, and omni-lateral responses to their world. Principals should determine in advance every office's range of functions, and in anticipating many of its encounters, prescribe appropriate actions in advance.

Appropriate in this case means effective, suitable, and profitable. These are all determined by the superior's or the sovereign's vision, the reason why its power and authority are extended away from its place of origination. Public offices may be classed as political, military, judicial, civil, religious, and ministerial. All are concerned with a dispatch, agency, or representation of the principal's mandates, government, and administration of public or divine affairs.

The Entrustment of an Office

A reputable and most effective office balances duty with responsibility, authority with accountability, and trust with dependability. It succeeds by discharging express duties and responsibilities. In relation to the Church, an officer: (a) *orders (b) sanctions (c) regulates (d) presides* over God's business affairs. Their spheres of service involve ecclesiastical, canonical, religious, communal, kingdom, redemptive, spiritual, natural, and heavenly matters for God and Christ. What does this mean? What is it to order something, to sanction its existence and operations? How does regulation come about through an official? What does presiding in an office entail, require, and rely upon? These questions should be answered by today's ministers so they intelligently communicate and properly execute their assigned mandates, mission, commission, vision, and ventures. Such wisdom is vital to the Ephesians 4:11 officers' fruitful occupation of their posts. This strengthens their ability to explain who and what underwrites their divine ministry agency and that it was received from God. Ministers should be well versed in how their office is to be exercised by them and over others in the interest of protecting and stabilizing the Lord's best interests in the planet. This is vital to a minister's credibility and cooperation.

Why Offices Persist

An office exists for the fulfillment of a vision, the execution of a plan, the pursuit of a cause, or the success of a tactical operation. Visionaries, leaders, executives, and builders could not accomplish much without them. To stand in an office is to carry out its aims, purposes, activities, and operations. It means seeing that specific tasks are performed. Offices necessarily maintain or expand a work begun and then enable the obedience, cooperation, duty, commitment, responsibility, and accountability that see to its fulfillment. For this reason, initiative figures prominently in an officer's service. It is an invaluable quality for the position to prosper. Every official organization must integrate a business into its operations. An income-producing, expense-generating component must be related to every office in order to assure the economy that guarantees productivity and prosperity.

The high point of an office establishes the primacy of correctness, propriety, authority, government, and order. A systemized form of God's government structures the organization. This calls for execution (follow through), standardization, uniformity, and maintenance (follow up). Official regulations are enforced by the staff of officials, agents, or clerks that processes its affairs. Moreover, offices today depend upon some type of facilities even if they are home based.

During the Bible era, offices were not necessarily confined to buildings. Officials, being largely nomadic and away from home, often resorted to portable offices to set up new organizations and conduct business in the fields. For this reason, the office was recognized as being embodied in the person. Its business was conducted in rural areas often in open fields. Tents were set up and tables were used to confer on official business away from temples, palaces, and courts. Here is how the office attracted the idea of being more of a sphere than a place.

Times have changed. Today's offices rely on other resources to accomplish all of its missions. These resources may be plants and facilities, equipment and materials, personnel, and other possessions seen as attachment to the officer's person. Recorders, processors, technicians, buying, selling, management, transmission, conveyance, communication, development, research, reputation, management, planning, directorship, and coordination are additional elements of the official execution of someone else's affairs and interests. Including these naturally brings in leadership, management, and administration—spiritual, natural, eternal, and temporal.

For the Ephesians 4:11 group, the "other" in the above description is **Christ and His affairs**. His officer's activities center on the Church. The mission is the advancement of the kingdom of God. The mandate is to *"Make ready a people prepared for the Lord."* How? *"Go ye into all* *the world; preach the gospel; make disciples; baptize and teach disciples, and then equip, stabilize, and unify them."*

Exercise: Take the preceding information and use it to establish the importance, purpose, and functional value of the five-fold. Be explanative and illustrative. **Discuss as a class or study group, if applicable.**

CHAPTER SEVEN
One Office Per Vessel

Chapter Topics:

Creation Manifests Divine Order • God's Creation Controls Human Pursuits • Perception, Attitudes, Other Signs • Creator Design Limits Arbitrary Ministry • Ministry & Minister: A General Survey • A Biblical Concept of Official Divine Service • How the Human-Divine Relationship Began • The Ministry from the Priest's Office • Biblical Terms Depict an Office • Divine Office Applied

---

I n previous years, the doctrine of ministry office universality has taken hold and run many ministers off track. Leaders and front runners of the last several decades so feared religiosity, order, and the call for criteria and rank that they dismantled the vital functions of a very good organization, the Church. The Church has fallen victim to extreme liberty and has consequently brought about libertinism, liberty taken to the humanist extreme. Proverbs 19:18, with broken restraint and perishing saints rampant among its members, has taken effect. Impulsive reactions to established religion, not entirely ignited by Christian frustration, fueled a revolt against order and structure that set in motion the church's preset downward spiral. Sadly, neither fear nor retaliation makes good motivators for change. Similarly, anger at predecessors' failed efforts is a poor tool for repairing their damage. Historically, fear and retaliation release an extremism that eventually displaces the original problem with another.

Often the removal of barriers, guardrails, and firewalls from ecclesiastical orders yielded a very dangerous fruit. Radical change is always risky, but sweeping elimination of what holds a foundation together is dismantling. Those initiating such eliminations may have thought through their reasons enough to benefit from the change, but rash liberation invariably succeeds in affecting other essential boundaries down the line. The heirs of this legacy are not faring so well two or three generation later.

Lack of enlightenment evidently led earlier leaders to believe no boundary is drawn between the church's officers, their offices, and other members of Christ's body. Since God's resources are mainly spiritual, popular teachers and scholars treat them as non-existent or intangible. Believing God sees things as they do—out of sight, out of mind—people are educated to ignore His fundamental premises governing all creation. That premise the apostle Paul told the Romans is clearly understood by what may be seen throughout creation's governmental order and hierarchical structure that permeate every aspect of God's visible creation. The mere fact that Paul could write about thrones, dominion, powers, principalities, rulers, and spiritual hosts in high places is significant. What do all these mean but that creation is an ordered hierarchy? Review the following passages of scripture for confirmation:

1. Psalm 97:9

2. Titus 3:1

3. Colossians 1:16; 2:15

4. Ephesians 1:21

5. 1 Peter 3:22

No matter what realm of God's handiwork and institutions you study, you find that boundaries and hierarchy are integral to them all. Jeremiah's prophecy in Jeremiah 6:13 is brought forward to Hebrews 8:11, further supporting this truth. God ranks not according to man, but according to His own callings, based upon His Creator foreknowledge of His handiwork. Despite irrefutable scripture evidence to the contrary, the church maintains a lateral leadership structure.

Creation Manifests Divine Order

God controls everything He made by His Creator knowledge. Being the intelligence behind all that is seen and unseen, He would hardly be a bright Creator if He simply made what He made and forgot how it works, how to repair or restore it, and/or failed to assure it serves His will. Darkened human creators would not be so dense, how much more the Lord of all creation. That is the rationale of this chapter's teachings. Every creation kingdom and its creatures have built-in signals to alert them to the Creator's will and desires. He put something in them all that confines them to His ordained boundaries, which are inherent in each one. Physical signals such as limitations, inability, weakness, and the like inform creatures of their natural limitations while particular strengths and weaknesses establish their place and territorial boundaries in nature's hierarchy. Flight, aquatics, and sub-terrains all serve these purposes. Natural restrictions sound pain or fatigue alarms to warn a creature that he is transgressing some border. Nature adds to these territorial boundaries, substances, climate, terrain, the elements, and indigenous inhabitants all join forces to signal to the wayward wanderer that he has strayed into foreign or dangerous regions. Early warning signs may be scent traps, water, rock or land barriers, or constructed barricades. Another delimiting sign may be subordinate guards that block the way, such as Eden's flaming cherubims that prevented Adam and Eve from returning to Eden's refuge. Any number of means is used to deter an intruder's invasion into another's territory.

Seen or unseen, respected or not, boundaries and hierarchy are built into all creation and they do achieve their purposes. Rocks barricade tidewaters, the sun blocks the night. Gravity guards the way to wingless human flight to seal the skies from fallen man. The invisible confines the visible and the supernatural, the natural. Spirits stand watch over the delimitations of the flesh to see that the mysterious treasures and privileges of the immortal world are concealed, protected, and accessed only by the shrewd or privileged. Every one of God's pathways has a door through which only the licensed and authorized may pass, and it is no different with the concocted institutions of men. They too follow God's order through nature's pattern. Doors, levels, walls, and barriers fix and keep their desired boundaries. Guards, alarms, alerts, and warning systems all shield space and not to be entered territory.

The secret to getting beyond the safeguards that preserve the privileged or private lies in several things: each one's physiological construction, knowledge, instincts, equipment, license, and genetic codes. These all, combined or separately, must be observed and correctly operated if one would proceed from a common space to a restricted one. For the animals, their construction is genetically encoded. Inner knowledge, instincts, and physical system intuitively guide or warn them about specific realms and territories open or restricted from them. By design they are licensed or not licensed to occupy or venture into certain areas. The same is true for the rest of creation. Ordainments are regulated and upheld by species design. Environments are blocked or released by Creator embedded patterns, programs, and signals to govern and orchestrate conduct and behavior accordingly.

God's Creation Controls Human Pursuits

With humans, the ruling principle of architecture and inspiration continue. Their pursuits too are largely controlled by Creator encryption. Musicians, actors, singers, mathematicians, and skilled people of all walks of life prove it. Either you have it or not, "it" being the ability that gives the right and authority to perform a function in a given field or business. Those who occupy an area will tell you that it cannot be manufactured and only slightly imitated. The supporting gifts and talents are either present or they are not and the decision is made by birth despite the argument about nature or nurture. While it is true that some activities can be learned or taught, there must be something there in the first place to enable the learner to apprehend the information. One can only nurture what, on some level, naturally exists and surface or strengthen what a person already has.

A natural talent cannot be bestowed by a teacher or trainer. It can only be nurtured if some seeds of it are already there. When it comes to organizational or functional hierarchy, humanity too is obliged to its laws and forces that are outside its control. These laws and forces are in keeping with the ruling guidelines set by God (see Job 33:16 and 37:7). The reason is that every vessel in whom is the breath of the Almighty never ceases to serve His intended purposes. He says this in Exodus 9:16; Romans 9:17. It is also voiced in Romans 9:11, 12: "(*For the children being not yet born, neither having done any good or evil, that the purpose of God according to election might stand, not of works, but of him that calleth;) It was said unto her, the elder shall serve the younger.*"

Human makeup, personality, temperament, abilities, and faculties divide and classify each special group. Whether they accept it or not, people's greater decisions concerning their existence have been made for them. Neither practice, frustration, deviousness, nor any other strategy can annul what makeup has predetermined a person is born and able to do. However, because we are so fearfully and wonderfully made, and God so seamlessly imposes His will on us, this statement seems errant. After all, people break their own records all the time. They learn new things at amazing rates and become routinely agile in unusual skills. The question is did God only bestow one blessing, ability, or talent per person for His callings or several to surface throughout a lifetime?

100

Once a person enters the world, does God cease to enable them, or is He able to continually, throughout a lifetime, upgrade and deposit special abilities for the ties that He needs in order for a person to fulfill destiny? Based on the manifestations they exhibit to the world, their life's work is cut out for them. The scientist may yearn to be an actor, artist, or singer, but his or her makeup determines if he or she can or will succeed at his or her heart's desire. The teacher may long to entertain; the mathematician may crave a chance at police work, law, or medicine. Still, makeup remains the deciding factor. When a person's desires disagree with his or her makeup, the stronger of the two settles the conflict *(1 Corinthians 15:10; Isaiah 68:4; Romans 9:21).*

Perception, Attitudes, Other Signs

Interestingly, people's view of a particular endeavor can say much about how well endowed they are for it. Special ability unsupported by accompanying zeal or drive are indicative. The limits of someone's immediate or cultivated understanding or appreciation of an action hints at how well suited they may be to succeed or excel at it. When redundant questions are constantly asked or instructions must be consistently repeated, it may say the person lacks the talent or knack for what is being taught or assigned, and God does rely on the abilities He deposited in us (Matthew 25:15). Enthusiasm, motivation, and interest further suggest a person's capacity for a subject or activity and intimate their predisposition for it. One who reacts with eagerness and hunger to a new idea or ability may exhibit the first signs of his or her propensity for it.

Beyond this is the stamina, commitment, and degree of instinctive or inspired understanding a person exhibits. These too tell how much a person is prone to its performance. A last sign is how often the person needs to engage in a particular activity and how long he or she can work at it; these may be summed up in, one word passion. Persistence, drive, perseverance, and determination are other strong indicators of a person's call to a certain vocation, activity, or calling. Attitude is just as important as aptitude; sentiment is critical to experiment; wisdom and instincts must work together to produce the right mix for any interest or endeavor; all are important to one's calling and achievements.

A newborn natural child's gifts and talents inevitably reveal who he is and suggest his life's work. The same is true with the born again spiritual child of God. The natural child may yearn to be a great athlete; her talents abilities and may say she is a born builder. The signals and controls governing the two fields may disqualify one for a chosen field or profession. Meanwhile once a person is saved, the new creation makeup may qualify for God's spiritual call although before redemption it did not, or vice-versa. Try as they might, Christians striving to be apostles or pastors, leaders, or administrators will find it is futile without the call to the office. Natural talents communicate entirely different messages regarding the performance abilities required for a divine calling. Spirit filled mental capacities, psychological outlook, physical stamina, even emotional perspectives may all shift a convert's performance potential upon redemption. What used to say one is a savvy entrepreneur before salvation may reveal a divine orientation to helps ministries, howbeit it advanced, despite the burning desire to preach the gospel.

The essential leadership aptitude may be lacking and the capabilities for the spiritual nature of the job desired even though technical ability may be present. In addition, the mental acumen and basic intelligence may all reveal the aspiration is incompatible with the makeup and stand up against the heart's will and not supply what is needed to perform or act when required. Lower creatures are compelled to accept this. Humankind, on the other hand, frequently rejects it in favor of its own will. The church is often like this.

The teachings that have persuaded the body to ignore or disdain God's ordinations show little comprehension of God and His basic orders. As Jesus said to the Sadducees who challenged Him about the afterlife with the woman who had seven husbands, "*You do not know the Scriptures, or the power of God.*" Modern teachers, too, do not always know the scriptures or the power of God if they fail to comprehend this simple heavenly truth. Purely carnal and earthly perspectives have confined teachers and scholars' insight and reasoning to life under the sun, to the world of the flesh. Consequently, a similar attitude causes modernists to teach the Lord's Church to covet what is not theirs and foster frustration and envy in matters that God alone keeps in His control. Desiring earnestly the best gift requires more than envy and covetousness.

To compound the problem, the boundaries and hierarchy we have been discussing are built into the requisites for the offices or ministry positions. The demands of the positions coupled with the need they fill and the purposes for which they were created all predetermine the makeup of the one to fill it. Pastors have specific functions. They possess the attributes, attitudes, skills, abilities, capability, and capacity to assure the job is well understood and performed. Often their life experiences further enhance their natural proclivities to see that they and their abilities meet the challenges of their ordained work. With the other E-4 officers, it is the same. Each one must "have what it takes." If he or she does not, failure is inevitable and the Lord's work will suffer; the minister's plans, purpose, and mission from Him will be frustrated.

Besides all that is the matter of understanding the office and their functionaries individually. If God endowed every creature with his or her abilities to capacitate a minister for His call, then one must compare the officer's talents with the requisites of the office. The functions of each position them must be clear in order for those to set the lively stones in their place, may say uniformly what gift, talent, endowment is best suited to the functions of an ecclesiastical office. A functionary is an official representative with rights, responsibilities, and privileges connected with the appointed position. The functionary is an operative who handles the affairs of a principal. He or she is deputized by the principal with proxy authority to fulfill the terms of the covenant. The functionary serves as the principal's steward or instrument and is used to set in order, organize, structure, and activate whatever the principal needs but is unable to attend to personally.

Creator Design Limits Arbitrary Ministry

As you can see from the explanations given, no one can arbitrarily decide to enter a principal's affairs without being assigned, and certainly not without asking first. Human leaders do not hire unqualified or incompatible functionaries and neither will God. They screen their workers and so should the church. Their screening policies put to rest the notion that anyone can choose or fulfill adequately and competently the office of his desire strictly on its own merits is false. The simple ability to carry a tune does not designate one a singer. To be argumentative or a debater does not guarantee a legal mind, and more than teaching a subject makes one a teacher. A pastor is required to do much more than attract a following. The prophet must be able to do more than see in the Spirit and utter words under divine influence. The evangelist needs to be able to do more than preach, and the apostle, more than found a work. All these offices have broad and varied functions that call for specialized skills and abilities.

Knowledge, intelligence, equipment, orientation, faculties, and capacity must line up with a person's natural resources for commensurate appointment and license to be conferred. Paul's repeated statement that he was an apostle by God's will, chosen before the womb and separated at birth for this calling, is quite suggestive. He claims apostleship before he is weaned from his mother, declaring his apostleship was authorized by God before he had never founded a church, preached the gospel, or was even aware of a man named Jesus Christ. What does all this mean? It means Paul discovered that his apostleship was not based on the obvious and predated any activity on his part. If this is true, Paul through Jesus Christ must have had other means of recognizing and determining who was qualified from the womb to do what. Considering he installed a significant number of ministers in varying levels of ministry positions over the life of his career, it would be naïve to think that he did so strictly on God's revelations. Recorded or not, he used more than instincts to assess and select his ministers and that is what we should do today. The question is, what would we use to determine who is endowed by the Lord for what post in His kingdom, and how would we identify and classify those endowments?

In later books in this series, the aptitudes a minister needs for a particular office are defined at length. From them you may discover if you occupy the right office or are suited for the ministry you feel called to fulfill. When thinking about the E-4 office Paul unveils, you must separate the office's mission from its purpose to see what reflects the achievement of its mission. Then you must identify the divine goal and objective of every effort and activity the mission requires for its purposes. Afterward, you should examine the position's description, its overall duties, fundamental responsibilities, and basic officiations and executions. Before you enter your ordained office or post, you should be reasonably able to cite these in their broad sense. Next, you should demonstrate an understanding of how you and your makeup fit in the scheme of God's plan for your office and your particular service. Then you should display a comprehension of the impact you and your work will have on Christ's body if you have the necessary natural, spiritual, and experiential qualifications. Finally, you should have a good idea of how your personal ministry methods, views, and inclinations will positively affect those you reach and teach for God. Some means of answering these questions should be sought and addressed before you step into that office you want so much for God to appoint you.

Based on all the variables and critical factors recommended above, you can easily see the problem with the popular idea that every minister can stand in any office he chooses at once. The present chaos and mistrust of the church because of it indicates that a method is not working. If the equipment is not there, then the prospects for success are nil.

Suggestion: Using what you have learned so far, do the following case scenario: Write a detailed explanation that explains to your Ministry Training graduating class why they are not sufficiently equipped to stand in the offices they desire. Include the limitations and other information that would preclude them from doing so.

Ministry & Minister: A General Survey

It is virtually impossible to appreciate the ministry, apart from thoroughly understanding ministers as Bible times knew them. The only way to recognize a class of professionals is to comprehend the origination of their sphere of official service. Doing so requires a spiritual, eternal, earthly, and professional eye. Much of the confusion over the church's offices and titles in the modern church has to do with its misunderstanding or disconnection from the Bible era's mind on a minister. In keeping with our theme, the ancients viewed all religious activity first as service to a god. They believed that everything they experienced in their world revolved around the gods. With this view, the word *minister* no doubt conjured up different connotations for them than it does for the modern, especially democratic, mind. *Minister* is the typical name for public functionaries discussed earlier that typically represent their countries abroad. This classification invests a functionary with a sovereign's character and mandates, and transforms the minister into the principal's essence and sentiment. Ministers represent governments and some are plenipotentiaries, those possessing full powers at their discretionary use, and greater distinction. All those employed by governments, religions, or the courts were ministers of their class.

Ministers were servants of divine beings, presumably or initially the beings that founded, ruled, and manipulated the physical world. No one in ancient times would dare renounce the idea that his or her ministry was a delegation from the gods. A sample of this persuasion is seen in Mark 11:32. Everything belonged to the gods by divine right and humans either inherited or were delegated their ministries by them. It was accepted that all earthly authority predated humanity and was part of creation's invisible governmental structure. Here is what underlay the Lord's parable of the vineyard and the slain son in Matthew 21:33-44. Although the Savior used earthly metaphors to convey His thought, His intent is pointed. Parabolically, He came to earth (the vineyard) as the landowner's son sent to collect His Father's earnings due.

Humans in the ancient world were subject to deities in the same way that the earth was subject to the heavens. Thus, for a dweller in the heavens to descend and appoint a mortal to handle a divine task required much to qualify the human. From fortifying the frail mortal vessel to augmenting and upgrading its lowly mentality to that of the higher worlds, the process is arduous. Here is what the Lord had in mind when He told His chosen to wait in Jerusalem until they were endued with power from on high. Those so chosen were called ministers, from the ancient root word *min*, defining one who gathers and presents a deity's due harvest. That the minister's first duty is to the sender, the divine being, brings in the other meanings of the word. The statements below explain them. A minister in the old world's mind is:

- A person authorized to conduct religious worship
- A person appointed to a high office in the government
- A diplomat representing one government to another
- A general minister ranking below ambassador
- The job of a government department head

What would happen if modern ministers put these key elements back into their understanding and execution of classic ministry service? Give the possibilities some thought and discuss them with others.

As servants of creation's invisible authorities accepted as superior beings, mortals were inducted into their divine service as subordinate officers that assist. Earthly servants as humans were the mortals that inhabited clay (Job 4:16-21). Their status in the governmental or administrative spheres of the earth was permanently configured by the gods, only temporarily entrusted to creation's inferior ranks or mortals. The human minister's status as a citizen of the visible world enabled the invisible one to employ them as agents in the flesh. A number of extraordinary benefits came with this detail, all to the end that the heavenly authority would have immediate and often ceremonial access to the planet through his or her human instrument. Another definition of a minister as an officer, depending upon the sphere of human/divine existence a person is assigned, gave earthbound beings rank in government, influence in justice, and say in earth's state of affairs. All this is included in a five-fold discussion to broaden your concept of what God has in mind.

Ministers, then, are God's representatives, functionaries of heaven's government sent to the courts or seats of human governments on earth. Our world being seen as a foreign nation in which the Creator desired to transact various types of ministerial business put them in the status of eternity's diplomatic corps, naturalized by God's Spirit upon or within them (see Nehemiah 9:30). In the church, that business can be limited to altar service, performing sacerdotal duties, or pastoring as a church duly authorized or licensed preacher of Christ's gospel. In this capacity, they administer His sacraments.

There are no less than forty-two synonyms for the word *minister*. That alone says the office is more than what we historically believed in the church. Some of the synonyms for *minister* include delegate, official, ambassador, clergy, parson and priest authorized to execute all the duties and access the rights to essential public ministry. Their Creator delegation gives the minister lawful access and legal right to approach the public in His official capacity. As such, ministers are empowered to initiate heavenly business on the sovereign's behalf, the premise of Jesus giving Peter the keys to its kingdom, or to intervene in public affairs related to the minister's divine service. They are first and always immediately responsible to the king or other supreme magistrate that appointed them. For the Christian minister, the apostle Paul says, "He that anointed and appointed us is God."

A Biblical Concept of Official Divine Service

"Ministry is the labor, work, and public service chosen worshippers render their god as attendants and functionaries acting on its behalf, performing deeds through divine offices ordained to benefit its masses and protect its interests" (the Author). Human ministers of Bible times were appointed as visible representatives of invisible sovereigns. Their duty was caring for, protecting, and providing for a populace the sovereign presumably brought into existence or won in combat. Ministry offices were attachments of governments, temples, and courts that delegated or assigned portions of the god's duties and responsibilities to those it owned or ruled. Ministers enable the public to understand the god and prosper in its land. They helped the deity to see to its people's needs. Ministers disseminated the god's standards of conduct and behavior and officiated over its acceptance requirements. They also voiced, mediated, and executed the god's judgments on disobedience and were categorized and legislated from the deity's world to humanity.

A Bible example of this is Jehovah's immediate etching of His Ten Commandments on the stone tablets carved from a mountain and given to Moses, Israel's new legislator. To continue, once enacted, the heavenly authority's legislations and will were divided and appointed to specific areas over which their designated human authorities governed or administrated. These declared offices could be priestly, royal, military, political, civil, communal, and were assigned as administrative departments of the deity's empire. Beside this was the nation's industry operated and maintained by humans under divine oversight.

How the Human Divine Relationship Began

Beginning with humans birthed or conquered by the deity (some were chosen) the specific spheres of divine service were impressed upon the physical world. Typically, these began with priestly service. First, the spiritual climate had to be settled and kept conducive to the ongoing transactions between heaven and earth. After that, usually came some form of governmental system, although occasionally this preceded or blended with the installation of a monarch. Royalty was originally seen as a direct human descendent of the god; Abraham and Jesus Christ are good examples of this. At other times, the divine being's royal lineage was interjected into a chosen one's genealogy to make it a royal dynasty such as with Saul, David, and Jeroboam. In either case, law and government soon followed or immediately preceded a deity's conquered territory.

From here, a host of public duties is distributed and maintained as finite aspects of the country's official obligations and thankfulness to their god. These, as said elsewhere, spanned the spectrum of human existence, from the 1) priestly, 2) ministerial, 3) royal, 4) public, 5) governmental, 6) judicial, 7) military, 8) academic, 9) domestic. From these come nine functional areas of settlement required for civilization: a) Organization, b) order, c) defense, d) parliament, e) adjudication, f) provision, g) industry, h) productivity, i) prosperity. These constitute official service. They were all, in the mind of the ancient citizen, the god's providential prerogatives for the land broken off and assigned to its populace by family line, geographical location, and divine destiny.

The Ministry from the Priest's Office

Motivated by previous discussions about the ministry, an office, and how both excel modern ministry's *gift* over *office* belief; the worshipper feature of the minister's definition asserts its spiritual inspiration. A key word in the discussion is *worshipper,* the immutable prerequisite for adequately serving one's deity. It is hardly possible to be faithful to something in which one has no particular interest or investment. The word *worshipper* brings the spheres of worship, religion, and divine service into the ministry scope. These all rest the topic on priesthood, the minister's direct service to a land's god.

Priests are those ministers that occupy a distinct, usually high level and class of ministerial service. They are the immediate intermediary between the deity and its people's worship. Priests are charged with seeing that all worship and everyone approaching the deity does so properly to guarantee community favor and a positive divine response to petitions and appeals for rescue, safety, and aid. Filling this position was the god's protectant for the people. The priests' intimacy with the god qualified their service and improved the likelihood the deity's desires were met as ordained. Priests essentially approve or disapprove, bless or condemn in the heavenly authority's name. The means by which priests acquire their vital knowledge and accreditation is by direct conclave with the god. Often intense orientation to the spirit world, its citizenry and the divine protocols that cover both conform the minister to the god's character and disposition on human life affairs. How the invisible world empowers and governs the deity's territory and operation is made known to priests in ways and contexts atypical to the normal worshipper.

From the rituals and sacrifices that best release the god's favor to what grants free access to his or her treasuries, compliance with the visible and invisible moral laws assured only blessings upon the land. These are etched in the priests' consciousness during the extensive education process. They see people always understand their god's will for them. This is presented in Malachi 2:7, "For the priest's lips should keep knowledge, and they should seek the law at his mouth: for he is the messenger of the LORD of hosts."

As you can see, antiquitous views differ greatly from how modern worlds understand religion. Early worshippers linked their worship to a literal being, not some imaginary spiritual concept or philosophical ideal. The ancient priest had little opportunity to renege on his covenant vows or to rebel against a religion disconnected from the god of the land. The being made sure its leaders knew they dealt with a person and not a concept. See Exodus 7:7-13:

> *"And he took the book of the covenant, and read in the audience of the people: and they said, All that the LORD hath said will we do, and be obedient. And Moses took the blood, and sprinkled it on the people, and said, Behold the blood of the covenant, which the LORD hath made with you concerning all these words. Then went up Moses, and Aaron, Nadab, and Abihu, and seventy of the elders of Israel: And they saw the God of Israel: and there was under his feet as it were a paved work of a sapphire stone, and as it were the body of heaven in his clearness. And upon the nobles of the children of Israel he laid not his hand: also they saw God, and did eat and drink. And the LORD said unto Moses, Come up to me into the mount, and be there: and I will give thee tables of stone, and a law, and commandments which I have written; that thou mayest teach them. And Moses rose up, and his minister Joshua: and Moses went up into the mount of God."*

Disobedience to the literal persona of the god revealed to the priests and leaders could cost a person his or her life. This was not only because the deity's presence greatly influenced national sustenance, but also that the presence could swiftly punish the priest or the community for dereliction or abandonment. Review 1 Chronicles 13:10 and Exodus 23:20-23. Lastly, there was the matter of survival; reread Exodus 23:22.

In a world, predating technology where energy, light, and motility were all non-existent, anyone claiming or demonstrating authority over these powers was revered and such a one held sway in the community. In an era where weaponry was yet archaic and the only thing preventing a rival ruler from invading a land was a superior army, exceptional geography and/or a powerful god-made divine culture was commonplace. Therefore it was quite easy, utterly compelling, to believe and obey a being that appeared out of nowhere in a blaze of light; that made visible objects (especially provisions) appear out of thin air; that seemed to have power over life, death, sickness and disease, or caused one's enemy troops to disappear or die without apparent cause. To be lifted up from the earth at a word, or empowered to coax or coerce creation to obey one's voice on the authority of a citizen from the otherworld were all quite alluring to the pedestrian era. It is what shaped their spiritual consciousness and enabled a reverence for divinity modernists cannot relate to in their faith.

The ancient world's problems were rarely easily solved and most crises relied on some type of divine intervention for resolution. All this, the ancient priests learned and were authorized by their gods to exercise. They freely exercised in their ministries their covenant god's powers and exemplified the wisdom to stymie the people and meet their daily needs. High Priests, those above all the rest, were closest to the god and delegated the highest authority and influence over the land. They generally received the laws and regulations first and in turn passed them on to subordinate priests to dispense to the citizens of the god's territory as recalled in Hebrews 9:6. This was generally done through orderly religious instruction, wise counsel, and punishment when necessary.

Biblical Terms Depict an Office

The following material is to present a snapshot of what an office means to the Lord and how He communicated His sentiment on it to His scripture writers.

> • 1 Timothy 3:13—The word rendered *office* in the New Testament is *diakoneo*. It means, "to be an attendant, spiritually a teacher; to act as a Christian deacon or minister; to serve." It is particularly tied to the office of a deacon and to its functions if exercised by one outside the office.

• 1 Timothy 3:1—Here the word rendered *office* in the KJV is taken from the word *episkope* for Episcopal. It defines "one authorized to conduct inspections, one that provides relief; a superintendent, specifically in the Christian episcopate." Concretely, episkope defines "occupying and exercising the office of a bishop." The word speaks to the office of the bishoprick, and as used in Acts 1:20 it comes from the Hebrew term peqqudah for visitation. The word does not mean a casual or social visitation but one of inspection, judgment, etc., applied to what apostles are assigned to do in accordance with Psalm 109:8. Furthermore, the word relates to Judas' fall from his office as one of Christ's apostles. Pequddah is defined elsewhere.

• Romans 12:4—Here is where Paul uses the term *praxis* for office. This word is most commonly used in the New Testament for deed or works. Strong's G4234, *praxis* (prax'-is) describes a practice, an act, a function, deed, office, work. Its definitions emphasize the occupational functions, acts, deeds, and work of that constitute an office. As Paul's eternal predecessor, Jesus too functioned as a *leitourgos* minister; one that is a public servant, a temple functionary, a gospel functionary, and a worshipper of God (it is always the result of being God's worshipper), a benefactor of humanity, and a minister. These all pertain to being occupied by profession as a public laborer working with and for the people that populate one's own nation.

Divine Office Applied

Office applied in the context of an activity relates to its target group, intended actions, or its most effective performance or treatment of general situations. The following points tell you how an office is applied and executed in terms of modern and scripture language. Another reference that ties apostleship to an office as used in the New Testament in addition to Romans 11:13 is Hebrews 8:2, where the type of minister Jesus is classified as in the New Creation Sanctuary is meant. The word minister in these passages is *leitourgos*, the very word Paul uses for his office of apostleship. Prototypically, it first identifies our Savior's ministry in eternity before it names His apostles on earth. The apostle, for instance, from Paul's inferences, is a leitourgos minister according to the Romans reference; Paul clearly understands this to be the type of minister his apostleship makes him.

A leitourgos minister goes beyond our traditional knowledge of the term's common variant, liturgy. According to scripture, it encompasses political, civil, social, and religious service to one's god or country. That the term is applied to the Lord Jesus Christ subtly

111

suggests that His ecclesia is more than a congregation, an assembly, or even a church as we know it. To God, the church is His kingdom, a mainly abstract concept to most of contemporary Christendom. Yet that is precisely the mien the Lord's gospel seeks to convey. Nowhere does it show up more vividly than in 1 Peter 2:9 where he designates the Redeemer's New Creation as a race, a generation, and a nation. Attaching his words to the Lord's brand of apostleship as an office, Peter's epistle shows the apostle's polity is God's everlasting nation. In our case, it describes the Lord's community of people in his first epistle. His understanding explains the basis upon which the apostle Paul uses the term in Romans 15:16: *"That I should be the minister (leitourgos) of Jesus Christ to the Gentiles, ministering the gospel of God that the offering up of the Gentiles might be acceptable, being sanctified by the Holy Ghost."*

The term, particularly ascribed to the apostle, is substantiated with Philippians 2:25: *"Yet I supposed it necessary to send to you Epaphroditus, my brother, and companion in labour, and fellowsoldier, but your messenger* (apostle –Strong's G652), *and he that ministered* (leitougos) *to my wants."* In this example, a young apostle is serving an elder one in the same capacity that Paul served Jesus Christ. Here is where the use of the word *minister* is downplayed in modern translations. Their renderings appear to overlook the public and political service aspect of ministry, limiting God's ministers' service strictly to the official assignment of gospel preaching rather than the expanded details that apostle Epaphroditus handled for Paul in support of both their apostleship. This was understood by the writer.

CHAPTER EIGHT

Characteristics of Offices, Officers, and Personalities

Chapter Topics:

Problem of No or Poor Office Criteria • Bible Examples of Criteria •
Table of Officers & Offices • God's Old Testament Pattern • Human
Instincts Insufficient for Office Recognition & Placement • Officer
Features & Office Functions • Differing Outcomes Require Different
Objectives

T he information contained in this section relates to all the officers. Refer to it from time to time to refresh your memory on the importance of the officers and the benefit of knowing their identifying features. Doing so will help you recognize the various representations witnessed in an officer's ministry as compared to the work done in ministry. Here the gift-office controversy is better addressed. After our extensive coverage of a minister, office, and titles, it should be easy for you to see the place of characteristics in a minister's calling.

A conflict between a deed, especially its excellence, and a duty is resolved for those that want to hinge ministry performance on qualifications plus talents. A disparity between the two could signal a servant's misapplication of his or her gifts, or a misjudgment of his or her call. Possessing the talent for something does not, on its own, guarantee other vital qualifications exist to manufacture a person's prospect of satisfying an office's demands. Another critical factor in the determination is whether the characteristics of the position are evident as well.

A characteristic is a distinguishing mark or feature that sets one thing apart from, usually above, another. It is also a called a trait. A collection of traits identifies a particular quality, a distinguishing feature possessed or exhibited by a thing or person that reliably identifies it. In discussing God's Divine Order, the characteristics that set one apart from the others are consequential, especially in light of modern teachings on the subject. If you read the previous material carefully, you understand how features make one a prophet, an apostle, or any one of the other officers of the church and how they are inborn. God implanted them in people's seed (genealogy) before the world was founded to define and influence their personal makeup by Creator design. In regards to the E-4 officers and the positions they occupy, God's predestiny bestowals can resolve key concerns over their respective capacity for an office. Essentially, it all has to do with solid recognition ability that can only come from uniform criteria that distinguishes one minister and ministry from the others.

The church God ordained must be able to recognize her leaders. She must be able to say with reasonable certainty who is the apostle, who is the prophet, who is the evangelist, pastor, and teacher. Such declarations must be based upon more than a subjective word, an unverifiable instinct, or a vague claim blamed on the God's Spirit. To satisfy today's more enlightened and educated Christian office, identifiers will need more than a repetitive unction in principle, not that these are unreliable sources for initial revelations. If the Lord intended us to look exclusively to our individual inner feelings and perceptions about these professional matters pertaining to His church, considering their fluidity, He would not have moved the scribes to pen the Scriptures. Apparently, the Lord found fault with our relying solely on our intuition, private interpretation, and inward unction as a Body to verify and place our eligible leaders.

The fault God found was with the instability of human responses. He saw that circumstances, external influences, even physical maladies could distort human perspectives and make their decision and evaluation undependable. What was clear yesterday or last week today for any reason may not be so clear. When it comes to judging the officers of the church, this is especially true. A number of things can trigger error or cause one to recant an announcement of who and what a person is in the Body, and in what stead he or she is ordained by God to minister. Aside from those just mentioned, other unsettling reasons human perceptions are insufficient for announcing whose who in an office may be strife, envy, a rift due to arguments, favoritism, or

114

just plain dislike for the person to stand in a particular office. The human factor is what it is, and it can greatly cloud the objectivity necessary to classify accurately someone for an E-4 office.

How many of us have been stunned by a visiting minister's assertion that someone in the church is called to or should occupy the office of XXX when we know them well enough to say that could not happen, at least in this lifetime? The present restoration of the apostle and prophet's ministry has suffered this a great deal. Itinerant apostles come in, and seeing a pastor that has a great, usually prosperous work, they conclude on sheer observation many times that the pastor is really an apostle. The same thing happens when a person gives an especially electrified prophecy. Based on the word alone, the person is declared a prophet with no other distinguishing characteristics displayed than a public address. No other criteria is used to make the call except their impression with the pastor's work. Those hearing they are now apostles or prophets are often thrown into a panic or into utter confusion at the news. If the itinerants were asked what they based their declaration on, the answer is usually because the pastor founded a work and the prophesier brought forth the word of the Lord. With the present church lagging way behind the early church in divine wisdom, culture, and ministry simple observations may not be enough to confirm a person's official call, considering how cosmopolitan the modern church is at present.

Problem of No or Poor Office Criteria

Objectively recognizing or placing a five-fold officer is especially hard when there are no established criteria to guide the deliberation and decision making process. In the absence of such criteria, subjectivity and bias usually abound as personal attitudes, theology, and beliefs can contaminate deliberations. For Christians, this contamination is often legitimized as scripture canon or at least inferred divine influence to compel agreement or acceptance of the word. Since there are no uniform criteria to substantiate these statements who is to challenge it? The church leader says God told him or her to appoint someone to a position, which may be true, but those aspiring to the post cannot agree unless the Lord voiced His decision publicly and they were part of the process. They have no guidelines to qualify those chosen and find it difficult to do so, on the unction of personal impression. For these people, disqualifying themselves is hard since they too feel as capable, yet they must rely on their human leader's words.

For a time this may be good enough until it occurs too frequently. God, on the other hand, used a public prayer gathering to anoint and appoint His leaders. When the Lord chose two ministers in Acts chapter thirteen, there were many witnesses. After a season of fasting and praying He called for the church to separate for Him Saul and Barnabas to what eventually became their apostleship. Jesus, before He chose the twelve, called for all the disciples and from them He selected those His Father told Him would be His apostles. See Luke 6:13.

In most contemporary cases, however, it does not happen that way as people are routinely installed in positions impulsively. Observers witnessing the practice question their leader's objectivity—justifiably or not—after watching several novices rushed into position without the training or proving they know the scriptures recommend. God has a peculiar biblical pattern for allowing this to happen if one subscribes to His alpha and omega omniscience of earthly life. God spends inordinate time training and grooming those He intends to use a long time. They are put through usually decades of pruning and proving before He installs them into His service. One can see this pattern with Abraham, Moses, David, Joshua, Jesus, Paul, and many others. All these giants took decades to ascend to their positions. That is not the case with the others; Saul is a great example. The Lord did not give Saul any training and hardly any admonishment. He got no tools beyond Samuel's pouring anointing oil upon him. After that Saul was abruptly shoved into kingship, sent to win wars, and stabilize a nation. It took Saul, according to 1 Samuel 13:1, two years to get it all together and begin to operate as king. He was, it seems, left to learn his position on the job.

A few bold souls ask the standards by which a particular office is filled, wanting to know how to fulfill their destiny in the church. However, more than a few leaders are at a loss to explain satisfactorily to the intelligent inquirer the basis for their leadership choices. Usually they adamantly contend that the Lord made the choice and they just obeyed Him. At this point, the member must rely on the leader's credibility and accept the answer at face value, press for a more definitive response, or simply abandon the matter altogether. On the other hand, what if the leader could produce a minimal profile showing how they conducted their decision making process? How responsible would such a leader appear before their constituency? What if a training record showing the results of a capable appointee's readiness and qualifying process existed to demonstrate that as much objectivity as possible went into the decision after the person was identified to them by the Lord? Would that comfort those that feel they have no chance at fair consideration if their leaders are at odds with them? Would not this further minimize to possible, even if unintentional, bias that can imperceptibly creep into emotion-based decisions?

Once or twice, the "God told me method" may work to explain one's appointment choices, but over time, it just may backfire. Vague rationales for installing one leader in position while refusing another can only work for awhile. Eventually, questions implying bias as the primary motivation for doing so arise as a leader's fairness and integrity are brought into question. Many Christian servants today challenge the "Spirit led only" method of choosing leaders because they have no recourse when they think unfairness is at work. Many of them leave their churches with a bitter taste in their mouths wondering how greatly anointed leaders can succumb to the very injustices they exited the world to escape. Such attitudes can be reduced where characteristic; talent, quality, and experience criteria have been intelligently compiled for each officer. The wisdom and uniformity of such a tool cannot be over emphasized. Its use can alleviate any mistrust concerning a leader's choices for filling positions as they are circulated throughout the organization so everyone affected gets an idea of how ministers and servants are chosen, prepared, and placed in their offices. Why is it that more churches do not post job descriptions so their members can see the standard organizational guidelines for position placement and know in advance the qualifications sought for the best possible candidate? Somehow, the Lord managed to communicate these to His early church, though the later one appears to have discarded it. Review for instance, Acts 6:3, 1 Timothy 3:1-13, and Numbers 11:16. From Genesis 41:34, Numbers 3:10, 1 Samuel 8:12, Nehemiah 7:3, Esther 2:3, and Luke 22:29, it is clearly seen that diligent processes for ministerial appointments are a way of life in scripture. When it comes to today's church and its ministers, there should be no difference.

When the Lord ordains a person to the pastorate, what does He base His decisions upon beside His omniscience? Should not those installed in the office share some common eligibility signs with all the other pastors? Is it wrong to want more than another person's intuition to make such decisions? Knowing our all-wise God as we do, there are established criteria for the pastorate that link personality traits to the distinct functions of every office. These are strongly implied in 1 Corinthians 12:4-6 where administrations are distinguished from gifts and operations differentiated from administrations.

Bible Examples of Criteria

The most comprehensive biblical example of this is seen in 1 Chronicles chapters 22-27. It covers David's meticulous organization of the kingdom to pass onto Solomon. The entire ordeal covers resource gathering, human and natural, and contains qualifications for royal use. Ten common qualifications surface repeatedly in every position that scarcely have anything to do with talent or instinct.

117

These include 1) wisdom, 2) understanding, 3) skill, 4) ability, 5) capability, 6) loyalty, 7) courage, 8) strength, 9) might, and 10) experience.

Sometimes the Bible indicates genealogy is a strong factor; certain families were dedicated to specific functions. That means genetics somehow figured prominently in the talent pool as most reliable for certain services causing families to double as professional guilds, national divisions, or organizational departments. In addition, seven broad service divisions appear to be common: a) royal, b) tribal, c) judicial, d) financial, e) military, f) prophetic, and g) security defense. Each division had its share of officials staffing, or supervising it. David's model comes from Moses, Samuel, Saul, and a number of less influential leaders that preceded Solomon.

Following is David's official table of offices, duties, and positions for the kingdom he handed over to Solomon. No doubt, it is patterned after the eternal kingdom of the Lord Jesus Christ from the above mentioned passages of scripture. They represent the general institutions, industry, operations, and government of God's kingdom.

Table of Officers & Offices

Position Title	Department	Passage
Supervisors	General	23:5
Judicial Officers	All areas	23:4
Gatekeepers	All areas	23:5
Praisers	General	23:5
Public Service	All areas	23:4
Priestly Helpers	Religious	23:28
Worshippers	Religious	23:30
Tabernacle Maintenance	Temple	23:32
Priest's Attendants	Ministerial	23:32
Priest's Rotation Schedule	Temple	24:3

Priest's Leadership	Ministerial	24:4
Sanctuary Officials	Ministerial	24:5
Temple Officials	Temple	24:5
Scribal Registrar	Census	24:6
Teachers	Education	24:8
Military Service	Military	25:1
Military Worship	Military	25:1
Military Psalmist	Military	25:1
Military Maintenance	Military	25:1
Military Worship Leaders	Military	25:2
Military Band	Military	
Royal Prophets	Palace	25:2
Prophetic Minstrels	Royal	25:3
Prophetic Seers	Royal	25:5
Prophecy Singers	Royal	25:7
Spiritual, Prophetic, Academic Teachers	General	25:8
Gatekeepers	All Areas	26:1
Patriarchal Government	All Tribes	26:6
Wise Counselors	All Types	26:14
Inventory & Warehouse Security	General	26:15
Urban Watchmen	Security	26:16

Watchmen	Security	26:16
Highway Patrol	INS	26:18
Treasury Supervisor	Treasury	26:20
General Treasury Officers	Treasury	26:20-24
Temple Treasury Officers	Treasury	26:20-24
Sanctuary Treasury Officers	Treasury	26:20-24
Official Judges	Justice	26:29
Regional Judges	Justice	26:29
National Judges	Justice	26:29
Regional Overseers of Divine Business	Domestic Affairs	26:30
Regional Overseers of Royal Business	Domestic Affairs	26:30
Tribal Officials Religious Affairs	State	26:32
Tribal Officials Royal Affairs	State	26:32
Military Affairs Officers	Defense	27:1
Division Captains	Defense	27:3
Army Captains	Military	27:3-16
General Royal Army	Defense	27:13-31
Military Tribal Officers	Defense	27:13-31
Royal Officers Over	Economic	27:13-31

King's Supplies

.	Agriculture Official	Industry & Trade	27:13-31
.	Natural Resources	Industry & Trade	27:13-31
.	Transportation	Transportation	27:13-31
.	Livestock	Industry & Trade	27:13-31
.	Shipment & Delivery	Transportation	27:13-31

No less than fifty-five areas of official service and employment were installed by David for the last time in his monarchical career. What do you think they used to identify the best people to fill them? If you were sitting with David today making these decisions, what would you like to see as the talents, experience, skills, and aptitudes of each class or position listed above?

God's Old Testament Pattern

The Old Testament was localized in the land of Israel. All who would benefit from Israel's covenant had to dwell in the land, be a Jew, or become a Jew. Christ's kingdom, on the other hand, expanded Yahweh's covenant to the world so that anyone filled with His Spirit became entitled to its privileges and obligated to its laws. Paul in Ephesians chapter four calls them "the commonwealth of Israel," NKJV. Nonetheless, the ecclesiastical substruct of the Lord's kingdom almost precisely mirrors God's natural and supernatural worlds. The scriptures present more than a hundred professional positions that served the ancient world. How do you think they staffed them, especially at the higher levels? Certainly, there had to be some type of record kept on each worker, their skills and performance that were compared with a skills bank, otherwise how could anyone say who was skilled in what? Besides that, before worker resumes could be developed, there had to be some means of linking job function with worker ability to categorize the jobs and ascertain the best talent, skills, and experience for what work. That is the premise of this discussion.

When one says he or she is a pastor, those hearing the statement generate a particular image that centers on the typical pastor's performance, behaviors, and conduct as they have observed them. The church has been trained over time to look for the telltale characteristics that depict for them the pastorate. The same is true for the evangelist and teacher. One need only hear the titles and pictures pop into his or her head to associate familiar behaviors and practices with them to understand what is meant. The same cannot be universally said for the apostle and prophet. Outside their closed communities, few people can say what characterizes either one.

Most people have negative images of the apostles and prophets' offices that stems from fiery sermons denouncing their existence and labeling them as heretical. Sadly, this causes the titles of apostle and prophet to meet with raised eyebrows and dread by those struggling to decide if they should exist. Such reactions are the fruit of simple lack of information (or misinformation) and the absence of organized education on the offices. Still, all the offices need clear definition that depict as well as state each officer's qualifications and demonstrated signs of candidacy. The remaining three offices need less explanation, but there needs to be some type of uniform guide to help leaders and members of the body recognize, confirm, and select who manifest the most biblical traits for what office of Ephesians 4:11.

Human Instincts Insufficient for Office Recognition & Placement

The point of this discussion is human nature and composition. Since its fluidity makes it unreliable as the primary means of five-fold recognition for many reasons, methods that are more concrete are needed if leaders are to maintain their credibility and not fall prey to errors in judgment, or be accused of injustice. It is a proven fact by now that the task of identifying the church's officers and other ministers is risky without sound documentation upon which to base one's observations and conclusions. The Apostle Peter was convinced of this by the Holy Spirit and wrote in his second epistle that the most sure word of prophecy could only come from the Holy Scriptures.

Having already been committed to paper, there was little chance the influences that invalidate spontaneous human perception could affect them apart from the human heart and will. Once they made their accurate way to a person's memory and heart, God's words could be recalled by the just and used to confirm or refute questionable beliefs. Reading the Bible repeatedly refreshes one's memory and strengthens people's recall of God's truth on a subject. It allows one to recommit to memory what is forgotten or distorted over time. You might ask, what has this to do with the characteristics and features of those who stand in the Ephesians 4:11 offices? The answer is plenty.

The Bible arduously goes through the trouble of defining what it deems is acceptable character and eligibility credentials for the people who would tend or oversee God's flock. Jeremiah addresses what God expected from pastors in Jeremiah 2:8; 3:15; 10:21; 12:10; 22:22; 23:1, 2. See also Jeremiah 23:4; 25:34-36; 33:12; 50:6. Although

Jeremiah was called by God to be a prophet, he says in 17:16 that he was assigned to the sphere of the pastorate. *"As for me, I have not hastened from being a pastor to follow thee: neither have I desired the woeful day; thou knowest: that which came out of my lips was right before thee."* Jeremiah's eternal calling and appointment was to the office of the prophet; the Bible makes this emphatically clear. He was, as many officers are, assigned to the sphere of the pastorate. Here is a distinction many of those rashly altering people's apparent or ordained offices may need to consider.

One may manifest as an apostolic pastor, but that does not negate the fact that the Lord ordained the minister to the office of the pastor, despite his or her works exhibiting the features of the apostolic. Other criteria is needed for a perceived promotion or title change to apply. Likewise the prophet, Jeremiah's example shows that the ordained office can legitimately function within another's official sphere and not compromise the authority or obligation to the God-ordained office while serving in the appointed sphere. Samuel was called a judge, although his official title was a prophet. What this means is that Samuel was ordained a prophet appointed to the sphere of judgeship. Evidently, the prophet's sphere of dominion includes judgment, which we know from Moses' mantle. These thoughts were included to expose you to them for review, and God's comments on the human trait, talent, or characteristic that best qualifies for the office of pastor. If you prepared a composite sketch from the content and tenor of the stated passages, you would have the beginnings of a reliable profile of the God-ordained pastor. Another collection of passages is also helpful to your profile. Turn next to Ezekiel's prophecy in chapter thirty-four.

What is equally important when we talk about recognizing those who rule over us, as the word says, is knowing what to look for and how to weigh our conclusions about them. The ability to do this is critically important for all ministries, especially pastors who are most vulnerable to the problems erroneous identification can cause. Pastors are the ones who open their churches and expose their flocks to the itinerant officers of the church. A mistake in judgment could be devastating to those in their charge. Therefore, the information contained in this section can be invaluable in protecting the flock from the ravenous wolves who stalk it for prey. The discussion to follow on characteristics and features can go a long way toward helping pastors guard their flocks. It is equally important for apostles and prophets to know whom the Lord is installing in all the offices, as they are the ordained first line of defense against errant officers. Apostles are the ones to articulate the offices and accredit their officers. The prophet must confirm or predict a person's call or rise to a particular office. Both ministries need a source of confirmation to assure their words are accurate and thus their reputations for accuracy remain intact. To do this, a body of officer features must be tied to God's ministries' official functions.

Officer Features & Office Functions

Every member of the Ephesians 4:11 staff should be well versed in what makes each E-4 officer what he or she is, and apostles and prophets should be thoroughly versed in the fine points that distinguish one from the other. We should all be familiar with the minimum characteristics to be possessed by every official of the Godhead, and understand how individual characteristics are to be applied and exercised in office. Those destined to minister in Christ's leadership all display consistent attributes, outlooks, and approaches to Christianity, its life and problems that are unique to their ordained positions. In much the same way, a police officer, criminologist, or medical practitioner can be recognized (in or out of uniform) by his or her viewpoints, convictions, and conversations. God's ministers too can be discerned by others in the Body—and sometimes by those who are not by their responses, attitudes, preferred method, and fundamental views on life in general. Bypassing physical looks, body build, language dialects, even nationality, the Lord's deposits in a person for eventual service to Him emit a common eminence. The call to minister is lodged in the spirit and is exuded through the soul by way of the personality and temperament of the "called one."

Close examination can show how viewpoints on like issues are strikingly similar or dissimilar to differentiate one group from another. Comments about religious matters, God, the church, even the people that make up the church, are usually shared by the same minister group, and are often discerned by outsiders as well. People, for example, that are not saved can often detect a Christian and many of them can recognize a minister. To continue, ministry emphases, development focuses, and outlooks on how to sanctify, refine, educate, and overall mature the church can pinpoint the call characteristics of each group. The apostle may see it this way; the pastor may not. The evangelist is convinced this is the most important thing; the teacher disagrees. The prophet says that all that is needed is "so and so;" the others see it differently. Previously these perspectives, once seen as hotbeds of contention, can today be used as guides to diversity. They do not, however, take into account whether or not the potential officer serves the Lord Jesus Christ, which explains why the unsaved can still pastor, prophesy, teach, proselytize and apostolize. The gifts and calling of God that are without repentance and the predestined call attributes are deposited in prospective ministers' genes long before the womb. Salvation and Christ have little to do with a human's common equipment for God's call; neither does what they do with that call upon answering it, because they are without repentance. That means they are irrevocable.

Differing Outcomes Require Different Objectives

To detect who is called to what, one should require evidence of a commonality in talent, interests, and temperament. Evangelists, for example, will always see Christianity from a strictly salvation perspective. People need to be saved, they need to hear the gospel; Jesus must be witnessed and every encounter with a soul must yield the sinner's prayer as its outcome. Prophets also display their official characteristics. For them the objective is the believer's intimacy with the Lord. The prophet wants to do all to make sure the Lord's will gets through to His people and seizes almost every occasion to let the saint hear from God. Pastors must have sheep settled in the fold. Instinctively, they are troubled by wandering sheep and concerned about the dangers lurking to derail a Christian's salvation. Sometimes too indulgent, pastors go to nearly any length to church a saint. The teacher is zealous about knowledge. The Christian must be discipled, must know his or her God, and become stable, fruitful, and prosperous members of the kingdom. These the teacher knows come by fulfilling the 19th verse of Matthew's Great Commission.

Lastly is the apostle. The apostle must see in the born again, Spirit-filled saint a fulfillment of the church's redemptive role as new creation priests. Apostles understand the Christian's salvation duty to manifest as the Godhead's offspring, surrendering as God's holy habitation to the sway of the Almighty in return. The apostle is absorbed by divine order because this office knows the supernatural hierarchy backing creation; the earth cannot bend to its will. The apostle invariably starts with the heavenly and eternal to impose the earth's obligations to the Savior. The Christian must become Jesus Christ, period! In conduct, outlook, behavior, and pursuit, the Spirit-filled saint must progressively transform into God's Son. The apostle also needs the saint to cultivate control over every area of his or her kingdom life. The flesh must be brought under subjection; the mind renewed to Christ and the soul transformed thereby. The apostle's watchwords are God's sons and daughters, eternal, everlasting, obedient, sacrificial, submissive, and holy.

As you go through the remaining books in this series, here are some considerations you may want to remember when studying them. Ask yourself, what is it about a prophet's spirit (a term used by Paul in the Bible) that enables its presence to be readily detected by the discerning eye? Take, for example, the woman at the well. What did Jesus do to cause her to see Him as a prophet? How is it that one can quickly spot an evangelist? What about the teacher-- what mannerisms does he or she portray that causes one to ask if he teaches? The same applies to the pastors—how are they recognized? What is it they do or say that gives them away? Deacons in the church have even been recognized outside of Sunday service. The acute eye can spot them in an instant. How? Why? These questions are going to be answered in the texts on this subject to come as the distinctives that reveal and classify one officer are explored. Obviously, the Lord wanted to enable us to discern who was who, and to enable all His ministers for His service. To do this, we have to accept that He implanted certain distinct abilities that reveal them to others. Identifying analyses point us in the direction of His implantations and gifts, and away from personal bias and private interpretation.

CHAPTER NINE

Nature and Attributes of Christ's Anointing

Chapter Topics:

The Anointing's Apothecary • Anointing is a Resource and a Person • Dispensation & the Anointing • Dispensation Means Economy • The Anointing's Two-Tiered Dispensation • The Chrio Anointing: The Anointing for Ministry • Chrio vs. the Ministry Anointing • How Chrio Differs

A nointing is the word used most often to encapsulate the ministry's graces, virtues, enablement, giftings and abilities. Of late, it has become the catchall phase for anyone practicing New Testament ministry. Typically, anything charismatic is dubbed as the anointing, from one's ministry office to sermonizing, to witnessing, to going to work everyday. Any spiritual manifestation is characterized as the anointing, and nearly everything done by a professing Christian falls under its heading.

Most people entering the body of Christ hold a vague idea of what the anointing means. Few of them understand what it entails. Many simply accept it as a spiritual covering that causes ministers to serve the Lord and His body, and they are not far off. However, the anointing is so very much more, and to serve the Lord under His headship, ministers need to have a broader understanding of it for themselves.

Summarily, God's anointing is an express exercise or application of the supernatural faculties. The anointing describes the empowerment Christ dispenses to all ministers for His work and its immense labors. Gifts and talents say the minister is capable; the anointing makes that minister divinely able. It appoints, anoints, empowers, authorizes, and enhances the minister's natural self for the work of ministry, supplying the supernatural power that teaches and releases God's workers into His kingdom. The anointing is needed to render ministers' latent and mundane ministry gifts and talents "divinely" useful, that is transcendent from the mortal limitations of the everyday person. The anointing engages ministers' superior forces and raises their natural endowments to their place of efficacy, readiness, and reliability. A servant's natural anointing may or may not be suited to the proposed minister's historical or experiential abilities; in some instances, it may even attack them. When the person is born again, the chrisma anointing (unction) that makes him or her God's child is energized by what the Lord Jesus calls "power from on high" in Luke 24:49 and Acts 1:8. Once the Person of God's Spirit descends upon someone, what may have been impossible or mediocre begins to "click" with what the Holy Spirit summons him or her to do. When the redemption anointing taps into its divine excellence, it performs consistently above what the minister normally experiences, knows, and is accustomed to performing. The source of that tap-in is the baptism of the Holy Spirit that endues with power from on high. In brief, the anointing constitutes the Lord God's ministerial providence at work in those He dispatches to His ministry field.

The Anointing's Apothecary

Before going any further, it is good to enlarge traditional beliefs and expectations concerning the anointing. Routinely, Christian ministers limit their application and substance of the anointing to their individual gifts and talents; in their minds, it is self-bound. Once the Holy Spirit presents it to them, it becomes a matter of their will and their works. What is often overlooked is how those gifts and talents are compounded to be administrated through them.

In addition to the minister's gifts and talents, the anointing involves the Holy Spirit and blends with the minister's makeup, special endowments, personality, and temperament. It also includes the minister's life experience, lifestyle, successes and failures, passions, and pain. Lastly and often the least acknowledged element of the anointing is those supernatural agents deployed by the Lord to see to the minister's success. Their dispatched, long-term assignment and heavenly initiatives play as big a role in the anointing as all those personal qualities the ministers claims. Eleven ingredients go into what may be the *apothecary* (amalgam) of every minister's anointing. Take our Savior as a case in point. Jesus was baptized with the Holy Spirit, received the anointing of fire, and then driven into the wilderness to be tempted of the devil. The text says that He was with the wild beasts and ate nothing. Such an environment would not only be a worthy test of endurance and suffering but could devastate the emotions as well. It was at His weakest that the devil came and tempted Him, supposing His hunger and isolation had stripped Him of His divine resolve and commitment to God's service. Upon winning His contest, the Savior returned, the text says in the power of the Holy Spirit. His hunger, isolation, spiritual seduction, and conquest over the wild beast all became part of what confectioned His anointing.

For the Christian minister, the anointing relies on Christ's redemptive *chrisma*, the New Creation spirit given to those born again from God's Spirit, and *chrio*, the added power that comes from being baptized by the Holy Spirit for God's particular ministry call. This is seen in Acts 1:8 mentioned earlier and repeated in Acts 4:31 that yielded a completely different outcome. The first dispensation stationed the Holy Spirit within as signified by their speaking in as many national and supernatural tongues (1 Corinthians 13:1—tongues of men and angels) as He would. The second dispensation empowered their boldness to preach fearlessly Jesus Christ to a pagan polytheistic world with greater signs and wonders. These all fused with the early church ministers being to compound the reason the anointing is dispensed by God. The anointing in this context refers to that divine upgrade, refinement, and empowerment that renders the minister's natural talents superior for God to powerfully affect His Body.

The Anointing is a Resource and a Person

The anointing, being first the Person of Jesus Christ, is also how He flows. However, it is not limited to the Lord's flows, but being personality driven reflects His divine nature and character, His will, His moods, and His temperament. These all become one with those of His servants and are how the minister can quickly adapt and respond to what the Lord desires and instructs in various ministry situations. Doing more than touching the minister's intellect, skills, and competencies, the anointing is also affective. That is, it engages the minister's emotions, sentiments, instincts and insight in every assigned project causing head and heart knowledge to coalesce and operate as one. See Matthew 16:8; 22:18; Mark 2:8 and Luke 5:22. Also, look at Matthew 12:25; Luke 6:8.

Despite untaught novices' portrayal of Christ's anointing as erratic, juvenile, and irresponsible, nothing could be further from the truth. Christ's true anointing is rational, strategic, methodical, purposeful, and deliberative. It absorbs the minister's mental, physical, and emotional faculties, absorbing the whole of a servant's human resources to capacitate him or her for His use. The anointing dispenses God's capability for continual though often invisible targeted action. The anointing enlarges the minister's being so that the dual existence of them both, Christ's eminence and the person of the minister, cohabit and cooperate in the same vessel with the distinctives of each remaining intact (recall 2 Corinthians 4:7). With the anointing, routine ministry becomes dynamic and power packed.

Dispensation and the Anointing

The word *dispensation* pertains to a household or an estate. At first glance, one is hard pressed to see its domestic connection with active ministry. However, Hebrews 3:2, 5 explains it. What Moses built for the Lord was an earthly house that Jesus immortalized. David, Israel's second king, began Christ's royal lineage to pave the way for humanity to become God's royal household, as noted by Peter in his first epistle. It was called the temple (house) made without hands that became Jesus' eternal body. See Mark 14:58; Colossians 2:11; Hebrews 9:11.

By the time the apostles took up Christ's commission, it was understood that His household was one of faith. As part of Christ's inheritance, the Godhead powerfully enriched His holy human temple with every spiritual blessing in *heavenly* places, which is what the apostle Peter was given the keys to in Christ's Matthew 16:19 apostolic commissions. Ephesians makes it plain that everything heavenly and spiritual has been transferred from doomed fallen spirits to the everlasting sons and daughters of the living God. Ephesians 1:3 presents God's bestowal as our dispensation; 1:20 as position; 2:6 as the church's status; and 3:10 as its eternal exemplification of God's manifold wisdom. God so approved of Jesus, He put the whole host of heaven's powers at the church's behest and qualified it to share His unlimited inheritance as the firstborn of all creation. That much wealth and power naturally requires administration and that is where the terms dispensation, anointing, and ministry intersect.

Dispensation Means Economy

What Christ's dispensation administrates is Godhead's everlasting economy. That means that Jesus manages (stewards) the Creator's *nation* (1 Peter 2:9), *country* (Hebrews 11:10), *financial system* (Romans 9:23), *wealth* (Romans 11:33), *salvation* (Hebrews 1:14), *treasury* (Colossians 2:3), *business and enterprise* (Acts 6:3 NKJV), *resources* (Revelation 5:12), and *wisdom* (Proverbs chapter 8).

The word *dispensation* constitutes the Creator's living estate comprised of human souls and creation's abundance. Economy is the term that best fits because *oikonomia* (oy-kon-om-ee'-ah) is its Greek equivalent from which the word comes. The two terms specially refer to a religious temple's—in our case spiritual— "economy" dispensed (stewarded, managed) as part of a deity's treasury.

The Lord Jesus is that deity and His reward for Calvary is the treasury made of the whole of the Creator's handiwork. Nonetheless, what is dispensed goes beyond money. It includes eternity's powers, special abilities, special grace, favor and virtue, and extraordinary access and collaboration with creation's invisible creatures. Dispensation's definition exceeds the customary period of time or era meanings we have all become familiar with; connoting infinitely more than a season, such as the era (dispensation) of grace. Wealth, substance, powers, privileges, and possessions are all part of the word's provision (Revelation 4:11). They are the economy God's ministers should be aware of to enlarge their appreciation of His anointing. Adding dispensation and its substance to the eleven ingredients of the anointing introduced above expands its potential effects to heighten His ministers' appreciation of the anointing Christ dispenses to them.

A further connection between dispensation and ministry is found in the inclusion of the word *temple* in its definitions. The initial household explanation given above is now narrowed to pertain to a temple, which is how it fits the religious sphere. Temples are governed as well as managed and that brings in the concept of divine law, another reason for ministers. Therefore, in addition to governing, instructing, admonishing, and overall judging the church, other official duties of the anointed E-4 officers are the management, distribution, and accountability for the New Creation's heavenly and earthly commonwealth and lawfulness under Jesus Christ. A glimpse of this is seen in Acts chapter six when the apostles assign deacons to distribute the provisions of the church collected from its members for the common needs of the body and in Paul's statement of the goal of his apostleship, he understood was to make the Gentiles obedient.

The Anointing's Two-Tiered Dispensation

The anointing is dispensed on two levels: *the gift level and the manifestation level.* It is much like the general effect of the Holy Spirit's presence in our experiential lives versus His endowment of the minister. On the gift level, the anointing capacitates as well as supplements. That means it makes you able and makes space within

131

you to accommodate for what you do not possess for a particular duty or task. The anointing in this effect coheres with your natural talents, perfectly enabling them to perform, produce, and present themselves to the Holy Spirit on demand. The supplement aspect of the gift level fills the space created by the Spirit within the minister that Christ needs to possess and ready His servants for His occupational use to guarantee His success when they are called upon. This includes enlivening the dormant gifts Creator God deposited before birth, enhanced at salvation for His ministry later in life.

On the manifestation level, the anointing exhibits more of its own personality and superiority. The Person of the Godhead becomes more evident. Here the Lord's use of the vessel takes over and completely overwhelms it to execute or perform what typically is only done mundanely. This action of God's Spirit is no less than excellent. *"But we have this treasure in earthen vessels that the excellency of the power may be of God, and not of us,"* 2 Corinthians 4:7. Where on the first level the *vessel employs* the anointing, on the second and highest level the *anointing employs* the vessel, and every minister to whom this has happened knows the difference.

At this stage, the vessel is acutely aware of being caught up in the Lord's efficacious performance of an otherworldly task. Now what the vessel ordinarily does well, he or she now executes exceptionally well. With precision performance, adroitness, wisdom, and competence, the minister moves at startling speed, caught up in the work of the Lord skillfully dispensing what the anointing brought for those who came.

As though the minister is two people at once, God's servant is keenly aware of and highly advanced to perform that transcends every one of the natural limitations. It is as if the minister can almost watch himself or herself moving in tandem with the Spirit of God, unable to explain why or describe how. All the minister knows on this level is that he or she is amazingly facilitated beyond the natural physical and human self and rendered more efficient in action than normal. Beyond that, the minister cannot duplicate or repeat the act until the Spirit wills. Here is the rudimentary idea behind what Paul calls in 1 Corinthians 12:3-11 *the manifestation of the Spirit.*

What the preceding example says to the vessels of God's service is that the minister will ever need the Lord. He or she can never initiate independent of Him the performance of the explosive actions of the Spirit of God. Ministers will therefore always need the Lord, and will invariably rely on Him to assure their successful service union remains effective, and God and His Son continue to be glorified.

132

Prior to discussing the attributes, a discussion of the two types of anointing mentioned earlier follows to aid your apprehension of the material that accompanies it. Here we talk about the Chrio anointing.

The Chrio Anointing: The Anointing for Ministry

No words better describe the matchless empowerment God gives people for His service better than "the ministerial anointing." Under the *chrio* anointing, one finds an official mantle's near discretionary use of God's power and authority a standing ministry entrustment. This type of free rein is usually given to, though not exclusively, God's apostles. Chrio anointing categories include and involve miracles, signs, wonders, and special miracles, as well as increased intelligence, unusual wisdom and uncanny logic. Each of them is discussed under its own heading throughout this section, in particular, the ministry of the dunamite.

Often there is much confusion over the separate enduement God adds to a vessel once He has called him or her into His service. Popular teaching insists there is no difference between what the minister has and what God gives to all His children. At first glance, the argument for evenhanded distributions throughout the Body seems plausible.

At the least, it is comforting to those whose frail egos cannot fathom one person being more endowed than others. Proponents of this view feel the only reason God would have for making any such difference would be irrational favoritism, if they credit Him with making any difference at all. You see, humans cannot help but see God as unreasonable as His creation knows itself to be. Consequently, when it comes to the anointing there tends to be much error surrounding it. Christians overlook God's wisdom in equipping each member of His body for His service. A measure of His anointing, Himself, His Personhood, and His power is given to everyone in the Body of Christ. As Creator of all, He gives all His creatures a measure of anointing as well to do their jobs; otherwise, He would have a world filled with empty vessels. What must be understood, though, is that there is no one type of anointing because there is more than one type of function employed by God in the church. Therefore, it stands to reason that He dispenses varying degrees of anointing to His different ministers to furnish them with what they need to fulfill His call, and they are understandably not the same for everyone.

Chrio vs. the Ministry Anointing

The standard consensus is that whatever God imparts to make us His children is sufficient for everything else He wants done through them. It is held that the salvation anointing, **chrisma,** is comparable with the *chrio* and it is all we need to fulfill our ministerial duties. This fact is, frankly, that is not so. The two dispensations are entirely different in nature, quality, intensity, density, and action. Their intents are not parallel and their effects achieve completely dissimilar purposes. These differences account for the success of one minister and the crumbling failure of another attempting the same acts.

While God is no respecter of persons, He does regard His handiwork. He may not be impressed with our personal merits and individual achievements, but He highly esteems His own. On the basis of His predestiny, God initially gifted one person in one area more than another. One saint or group of believers He made more talented than others to perform in a given field. Extending this even further, God's variations are made even more pronounced upon conversion. Occasionally, the gifted one may cease to be outstanding in a pre-redemptive area because God needs his or her full attention and skill in another area. Meanwhile, the mediocre becomes suddenly exceptional in the very field the achiever once dominated. Why? The answer is the anointing to expedite the call of God; in particular it is the chrio anointing.

Many times the ministers' natural endowments are sufficient for their service in the world. However, for His ordained ministry purposes they are altered because entering God's kingdom, keep in mind, is a promotion. The Lord established His church above all principality and power (Ephesians 1:21) and so its labors are weightier and touch a wider sphere of creation. More than the natural, therefore, is needed for its accomplishment. The *supra* eternal is called for to enable the minister not only to succeed as always, but also to excel as never before. This is achieved through the anointing we have been discovering. God's supernatural outpouring upon a minister's vessel for work means previous limitations and hindrances are alleviated for the duration of the assignment or the end of the ministry. That outpouring the Bible calls the "baptism of the Holy Spirit." The baptism is for the *enduement*: empowerment that invests with power, authority, ability, license, and capacity for the work of ministry. This is not, it should be underscored, the same action as that which takes place when one is born again. Redemption imparts the qualities of the Godhead within by the Holy Spirit. Once the Lord slaughters the old spirit, He implants the new one within to make the convert His offspring, a literal child of God. Taking one's theological blinders off releases profound implications regarding this truth. A different process and different objectives take place when the Lord anoints a minister for His call.

To assure you have every opportunity to cease from sin, the Lord adds a measure of Himself inside to guide, strengthen, and quicken you to live and behave as His child. The event, called the New Birth, is foretold by Ezekiel in Ezekiel 36:24-27 and declared by Jesus in John's gospel chapter three. The word used for the action of the New Birth is *chrisma*. It defines God's **familial anointing** that is deposited forever when one receives Jesus Christ as his or her personal Savior. The process passes one from spiritual death to eternal life, from sin to righteousness, and darkness to light. Being made one of the Creator's eternal offspring in Jesus Christ is what 1 John 2:27 is talking about. It registers the new converts as members of God's new creation race of human divines made in Christ's image and likeness. Consider John's words in 1 John 3:2, *"Beloved, now are we the sons of God, and it doth not yet appear what we shall be: but we know that, when he shall appear, we shall be like him; for we shall see him as he is."*

What God does beyond confirming the call to ministry is equip for ministry. From the **facultative** reservoirs within Himself, instead of the familial ones, God draws strength, fortitude, skill, knowledge, and learning capacity, as well as enrichment for the things He needs His servants to do. Insight, wisdom, awareness, courage, and boldness accompany the ministerial anointing. In addition, the chrio anointing enables the signs, wonders, and miracles that distinguish the Most High's power from the rest. Chrio enables the healings, deliverances, restoration, and even resurrection the Almighty is known for to occur at the minister's word. This anointing is what Christ got when the dove descended upon Him as the very Son of God Himself. He certainly did not need to be born again; hence the chrisma anointing for Him would have been redundant. He was born sinless as the incarnate God. What He received upon His baptism by God's Spirit (a type of the ceremonial washing required of the priest) was power for service. He was possessed by the Holy Spirit to execute that which the Father had sent Him to do. The name for His anointing, then, is *chrio: "The Spirit of the Lord is upon me, because he hath anointed (Chrio) me to preach the gospel to the poor; he hath sent me to heal the brokenhearted, to preach deliverance to the captives, and recovering of sight to the blind, to set at liberty them that are bruised, To preach the acceptable year of the Lord,"* Luke 4:18. See also Acts 4:27: *"For of a truth against thy holy child Jesus, whom thou hast anointed, both Herod, and Pontius Pilate, with the Gentiles, and the people of Israel, were gathered together."* Helpful scripture references for these facts include Acts 10:38, 2 Corinthians 1:21, and Hebrews 9:11. Chrio anointing **consecrates to divine service** by furnishing the Lord's ministers with what they need for ecclesiastical and kingdom ministry.

How Chrio Differs

Chrio properties are heavier, more apparent, and more dominating. Chrio spurs you to act on behalf of God and supplies what you need to do so as needed. This anointing requires faith, commitment, and consistent action to work as it intensifies with constant use. Christ's words in Mark 4:24, 25 emphatically supports this truth. *Chrio's* main distinguishing features are authority, command, imposition, intervention, and density. Chrio is more effectual and demonstrates personality, intelligence, purpose, and drive as it simultaneously melds with the minister's own. Anyone who has ever been overtaken by the chrio anointing's overwhelming command by the Holy Spirit to do something can tell you the unmistakable and unforgettable difference between the *chrisma* and the *chrio*.

When the Old Testament prophets spoke of the anointing, it was *chrio* and not *chrisma* they had in mind. The new birth was not needed for their external vesting of the Holy Spirit's empowerments, only an ordination by the Lord. On the other hand, what was needed for the Holy Spirit to indwell them is something else altogether. Here a nature change must be accomplished. Until Christ, the legal ground for God to do this was not yet obtained. So the Old Testament prophets that spoke of being weighed down by the hand of the Lord, or being rendered supernaturally superior, were made so by the chrio anointing.

CHAPTER TEN

The Church's Manifestations, Operations, & Administrations

Chapter Topics:

How Important are Signs? • Signs Also Served Prophecy • The Bible & Miracles • Prophecy as a Miracle • Wonders • The Ministry of the Dunamite

T his chapter addresses some of the operations of the Spirit, such as miracles, signs, and wonders. Miracles, coming from the Latin *miraculum* and *mirari*, to wonder, were understood in Bible times as wonderful events that occurred by extraordinary means. They called attention to themselves by what they signified or achieved. The three New Testament Greek words for *miracles* are:

- *Semeion* – a sign
- *Teras* – a prodigy
- *Dunamis* – a mighty work

Brought forward from the Old Testament, the Hebrew words *'owt* and *mopheth*, as *semeion* for sign and *teras* for wonder, ended up as the Latin equivalents used in the Greek. See Exodus 7:9. Often God attaches signs to miracles that certified the Lord had commissioned a minister or messenger to His service. See John 3:2. The word *teras* stands for our word *prodigy* for "a wonder." Wonders may be events such a phenomena or a person such as a genius. The word may apply to brilliant people, high intelligence, outstanding ability, the exceptionally gifted and talented. The word *prodigy* emphasizes the effect or impression of a divine sign on those that witness it.

Dunamis identifies a "mighty work" normally performed by a superhuman power (Acts 2:22; 2 Corinthians 12:12; 2 Thessalonians 2:9). Signs seal God's attestation or proof of a revelation as really from Him. The Savior's miracles were wonders that served as signs of His power, divinity, and standing in the Godhead.

How Important are Signs?

Signs sponsor or ignite events, or natural phenomena override natural laws in order to expose an era and its people to the spirit world and reveal its God in the process. A sign is a visual wonder that betokens something else and can be a mighty act not performable by humans. Signs were well understood and often demanded in ancient times, especially in a world saturated with divine consciousness. Supernatural manifestations of divine power were a nearly everyday occurrence in some cultures and at various periods in human history. They were more common, and still tend to be, in pedestrian powerless areas where humans must rely on the otherworldly for their sustenance and to comprehend their world. Signs often were sent signatures of a divine dispatch as seen in Exodus 4:8: "*And it shall come to pass, if they will not believe thee, neither hearken to the voice of the first sign, that they will believe the voice of the latter sign.*"

In this instance, the sign's objective was to speak convincingly for God to those whom Moses was being sent. In the scripture, the voice is not only connected to a sign, but it is also presented as a means of persuasion. Thus, signs portray the power and authority that performs them and communicate with easily recognized imagery what is well known to a particular culture. Signs say what divine senders transmit through their messengers to their observers.

Moses' ten plagues themselves, all natural disasters, were called signs by the Lord. They were signs that Moses was sent by the Almighty, that He indeed wanted Pharaoh to let His people go, and that the Most High was more powerful than all Egypt's gods (Exodus 12:12). Every sign was calculated, deliberately chosen to engage the polytheistic nation's deities in cosmic battle. Hence, signs can be more than portents, events, or phenomena; they can be statements, weapons of war, and tools of persuasion, undeniably evidencing a higher power at work in the mundane. Such was Yahweh's intent when He toppled Egypt to show His power to a Pharaoh that He raised up for that very purpose, including in the contest the Pharaoh's very existence and rulership as part of His signage.

The signs themselves, our Exodus reference teaches us, proved to be the literal voice of God translated to action by the events they caused. In addition, how the world acts on the voice of God's word is seen in Psalm 103:20, where invisible creatures, God's angels, are how He performs the voice of His word. They are the unseen agents mobilized by the voice of God's word. See also Hosea 2:21.

Miracles were sought because they had no other recourse. Recall the world that invited and rested upon divine beings coming and going and you will see how essential a miraculous lifestyle was for the ancients. Miracles were how the spiritually dark and dead world that existed before Christ recognized their supernatural visitors and learned what it took to get them to act on their behalf. These were experienced from divine encounters with spirit beings that delivered special revelations of themselves and their powers. They perform as representatives of their deities or as the very gods themselves. Their goal was to aid, establish, preserve, or provide for their authority's purchased, conquered, or acquired possessions. At the least their manifestations attested to the spirit world and assured those on earth that they were not alone. Here is the spirit of what the Lord Jesus meant when He told those that He was about to leave behind that He would not leave them orphans.

Signs Also Served Prophecy

Signs also conveyed the language of prophecy, such as the sign of the hand that wrote Belshazzar's judgment on the wall in Daniel chapter five. Here the sign was a portent of some future event that the God that Nebuchadnezzar had given power over Babylon while on his throne. The only one that could read the message was Daniel, something strange in itself considering kings were typically multi-lingual to communicate with the numerous peoples in the land.

Integrating nature in their messages, which is most unlikely to change or be altered by humanity, signs emphasized spiritual features common to the most popular religions that people sought in their quest for truth and power in a powerless world. Signs alerted them of the divine beings' involvement in their world and oddly enabled spiritually dense humans to comprehend the supernatural's help in life's routine affairs. Man-made imagery was frankly distinguished from what God created, so there was no mistake in the ancient mind about what was enduring and trustworthy and what was transient. When temporality was to be stressed, then fabricated earthly emblems were used to indicate the sphere the sign pertained to.

When thinking about the importance of signs and their prophetic link, they were as vital to earlier travelers as those huge markers along the road guiding your journeys today. To greatly understand what signs meant to the Lord's prophets and to appreciate their importance to the Lord's messages, reflect on the signs and guideposts that told the pedestrian traveler of old where he or she was in his or her journey.

Those signs that comfort you as you drive your lonely unlit road at night were not there for the ancient traveler. They had to rely on the placement of a rock or tree or body of water to trace or retrace their steps. Similar to natural signs, prophecy helps you confirm your direction, desired path, distance, and location in life, warning you about dangers or delays that may lie ahead. Signs are invaluable to seeing that you reach your intended destination safely, peacefully, and confidently. You rely on signs and accurate mile markers to best time your journey and plan your stops. In the natural, you trust signs to tell you the next exit and the connections to the next highway or rest. In the same manner that the highway's name or number has to be correct, your recognition and confidence in signs must be, too. Those who traveled the road before you need to have correctly marked your road with signs that can be trusted to get you to your destination. God uses spiritual signs the same way, sending them at crucial times in life to mark your course, warn you of danger, and confirm your right direction.

The Bible & Miracles

Scripture is replete with miraculous events in the Old and New Testaments. They were called also signs and powers to designate their underlying motives, to signify or certify God's power at work in the world of men. The following scriptures chronicle the Bible's legacy of miracles: Mark 9:39; Acts 2:22; 19:11, cf. Exodus 9:16; 15:6; Luke 23:8; John 2:11, cf. Numbers 14:22; Deuteronomy 11:3. The New Testament wants us to understand that under Christ's dispensation, miracles served a deeper purpose and carried greater meanings. Many of those He performed, for instance, were fulfillments of the Old Testament miracles that foretold His coming. Others were signature events that confirmed the Messiah had indeed arrived on earth. As astronomical as it was for the host of angels to appear in the sky announcing His coming to earth were the very miracles He performed to identify Himself and unfold His redemptive plan for humanity. Christ's first advent in itself changed time by winding down the adamic era and igniting that of Himself and the church.

As powers, miracles are also called in scripture mighty works, such as those Moses, Elijah and Elisha, the apostles, and especially Paul were known for performing. At other times they are referred to as wonderful works, as recognized by those dwelling in Jerusalem hearing those in the upper room speak in other tongues as the Spirit gave them utterance. Those who heard the sound understood their words to be declaring the wonderful works of God in Acts 2:11. Summarily, miracles have as their one standing objective, the manifestation of God's power, even if He chooses to do so through one of the many agents He put at His disposal. As stated elsewhere in this book, they are executed by God's Spirit and are dubbed as "the finger of God." Miracles, however, are never an end in themselves; they invariably aim to direct the observer or beneficiary to something beyond himself or herself and intend to establish that God is near at hand. In the New Testament, miracles mean to express the presence of God's kingdom in the planet.

More than just saying that God is visiting His world, New Testament miracles convey that His kingdom by His Spirit now resides in the earth and may be exercised by those that know the secret to releasing the Creator's power. That is why Acts 2:17 says God's Spirit is poured out on all flesh and as a result, each one will prophesy, see visions or dream dreams. It is implying that the Holy Spirit in the planet becomes its dominate source of spiritual power and will affect, as He woos everyone to salvation, all those that enter and dwell on the planet. The text does take time to say that the effect of the Holy Spirit on God's menservants and maidservants is different, apparently coming from a different stream of His power. Their prophesying would be about Him and not just anything spiritual in general. Whatever the case, the object of God's miracles in the planet is to affirm His reconnection with His planet and renewed dominion over the works of His hands. They may release His voice, divulge His mind, exercise His power, impose His will, attend to His affairs on earth, or merely deliver a message in the form of a sign. Miracles also mark those who are in the Lord's service so that His authority at work in them is regarded. See for instance, John 2:18,23; 3:2; Matt 12:38; Acts 14:3; 2 Corinthians 12:12.

Miracles always intend to work the works of God. God uses miracles, signs, wonders, mighty works, wonders, and wonderful works to intervene in His established creation order. They allow Him to circumvent His order providentially as part of His intercession on His creature's behalf. A miracle is a visual appearing of what was and is normally unseen. It imposes Creator desires and initiatives on the natural world by extraordinary and supernatural means. Exhibiting more than God's power, they show forth His omniscience, wisdom, omnipotence, and skill. God works His wondrous works to cause people to marvel and to remind them that their worldly best is still quite insignificant in the creation's overall scheme of life. Miracles reflect the Creator's divine powers as the Godhead. They demonstrate His supremacy by special acts that regularly let humans know they are weak, and they show His complete liberation from what binds humanity in the earth. Miracles reveal God's dominance in the Lord's higher orders and authorities at work in the realms and spheres of humankind.

Scripture introduces Moses as the first of God's miracle workers. That is not to say the Lord worked no miracles before him. Noah's building of the ark and Abraham's slaughter of the five kings at God's inspiration, for instance, are also miraculous in nature. Neither man could have, on his own, accomplished such monumental feats. What Moses introduces to us is God's collaboration with a human to impose His divine will upon creation apart from His apparent assistance. God dispensed to Moses enormous powers to accomplish his delegated task and trusted the prophet to work that power at his discretion. God authorized Moses to recall the plagues he released and intervene in their destruction for God's mercy on Egypt's behalf when Pharaoh feigned repentance. So discretionary was Moses' use of God's power that when he was angered by the people at Meribah, he sinned and recklessly hit the rock that God expressly told him to speak to for water, so Israel would hallow their God for quenching their thirst.

The next most memorable exhibitions of God's miraculous power were performed by Elijah and Elisha. Their entire ministries were saturated with the supernatural to demonstrate for Israel God's power always at work in them. The Lord used miracles to help His people believe His revelation and honor His truth. To accomplish this purpose, the Lord strategically worked miracles in times of great upheaval, shifts of power, or in great crises of national faith and survival. True miracles aimed to affect the senses and impress the heart, intellect, will, and conscience with God's realities. When the Lord founded the church, He did so with miracles as a powerful display of the same God that birthed natural Israel.

From Pentecost to Paul's special miracles, the Holy Spirit showed Israel's God to be the same, yesterday and forever. He came upon His people with great strength in Acts 2:1-13, converting thousands to His new kingdom. Christ's power extended to His ministers, like Philip the evangelist, whom He anointed with powerful signs and wonders. His special miracles accompanied every call to apostleship. The book of Acts records Peter's passing shadow was strong enough to heal the sick by merely overshadowing the infirmed to display the potent signs and wonders unique to His apostles. The most concentrated expression of God's miracles, according to Acts 2:43 and 4:33, were Christ's apostles, as miraculous powers were His way of authenticating them for the church. So special were the apostles' dispensation that they alone were credited with the privilege of transmitting their miracle working power to others. Usually this was done by the laying on of hands.

Prophecy as a Miracle

Previously, we linked prophecy to signs to show how they facilitated the Lord's transmission of His word. When it comes to miracles, the same is true. Who would not call the voice of the eternal immortal God breaking through the sound barrier to be heard by humans a miracle? Prophecy is just that, as much as is the God of all creation deciding to reveal His mind through a human being. It can be said that prophecy is one of the greatest of all miracles; it is certainly one of the most consistently performing ones. Most miracles are performed once and rely on visual recall to be recalled, that is not the case with prophecy. Biblically speaking, miracles are generally not repeated. The most dramatic of all prophecies is that of Christ's Messianic office manifesting as prophetically foreshadowed in Scripture. The miracle of prophecy is how the people of His day knew the long awaited word of the Lord had come to pass in the Person of the Man from Galilee. Genesis' promise as spoken by the Creator directly to Adam and Eve happened as His Messiah finally appeared as vividly depicted by Yahweh's prophets. Just as they progressively introduced Him from the beginning, Israel's Messiah arrived, worked His foretold signs and wonders, and exited the planet as they foresaw centuries ago. He performed prophecy-fulfilling miracles, exercised divine power, and delivered the message the Creator prepared the world to receive as God's perfect sacrifice, sent to take away the sin of the world. See Luke 24:27.

Wonders

Of the words introduced in this chapter, the least mentioned word of the four (signs, miracles, dunamis, and wonder) is the word *wonder*. This Greek rendering of *wonder* is the Hebrew term *mowpheth* mentioned above. A wonder is a conspicuous work taken to be a *miracle*, according to Exodus 4:21; 11:9. When the word does occur in the Old Testament, it is usually paired with the Hebrew term *'othoth—owt* above—meaning signs. A synonym for *wonder*, to depict its effects, is the word *marvel* for instance. In this sense it is recognized in the Hebrew as the word *pala'* or *pele'*

The New Testament employs the words *thaumazo* and *teras*, the other word introduced at the beginning of the chapter. Aside from meaning marvel, it refers to a portent; an omen, sign, warning, indicator, signal or augury. All these words, you can probably deduce, relate to prophecy. Here is what the Hebrew writers essentially had in mind in the application of the word *pala* to extraordinary occurrences. Wonders have the evidential effect of separating the normal from the abnormal, the heavenly from the earthly, and the human from the divine. Their appearance clearly declares that the supernatural has intervened in the natural order of things. These could be attained by deeds, natural phenomena, prodigious people, or auguring events.

The Ministry of the Dunamite

Coming from 1 Corinthians 12:28, 29, this discussion addresses another ignored office of the New Creation church. While verse 28 of the passage does not divulge it plainly, the next verse definitely does as it refers to the miracle worker, or what we have termed here, the dunamite. The newcomer to this revelation will be amazed to learn that the Lord appointed among the standing officials of the church, the *dunamite*. The implications of this truth is enormous. What makes this minister unique is that he or she occupies and routinely exercises the sphere of the impossible in God's New Creation church ordainments. Imagine the Lord ordaining and endowing a force of humans to operate continually His miraculous spheres to manifest easily the normally unattainable for those in the local congregation. This minister is the stationed finger of God on staff in the church.

The dunamite is the one with extraordinary faith, spiritual power and insight, and an instinctive consciousness of the demands to be put on the spiritual world to force it to release its holdings into the earth. The dunamite is a warrior, a wise counselor, and a power-wielding weapon in God's camp. He or she is likely to appear as a mental giant because of the potent fusion of the spiritual to the natural mind, grasping the supernatural and effortlessly tapping into its mysteries; skillfully penetrating its barricades to maneuver and provoke the physical manifestations of its buried treasures. Their accomplishments are not confined to money or physical healing alone, but effects anything the invisible world withholds from the earth. They may provoke all health, ability, possession, spiritual enlightenment, and enrichment. The closest Bible portrait of this minister is seen in Luke 9:1; Matthew 10:1; Acts 8:6, 13. Bestowed most frequently on apostles, the New Testament shows that evangelists too exercise this mantle. However, that the Lord mentions the dunamite as an official position suggests that it is an official mantle that can function independent of the other ministers.

Dunamites have insight, keenness, and authority to go and retrieve verbally and personally all God said He has given to the children of men; meaning by this, humans. They are God's secret agents of power, provision, and invocation who are authorized to access those spiritual blessings in heavenly places more readily than most other members and ministers of the church. Until recently, the dunamite ministry has been unheard of and untapped in the church. The Lord ordained His church be endued with supernatural powers and efficacy endowments to fulfill its multifarious callings and facilitate its expansive missions. His enduement strengthens those who fill the positions in the Church continually. The heretofore overlooked ministry of the dunamite does exist, even if the office has been vacant and is soon to be revived and occupied today. Nothing in New Testament scripture indicates the Corinthian ordinations were to be done away with or interrupted for any reason, so they must continue as long as the Church remains on the earth.

CHAPTER ELEVEN

Ministry Class Notes: Covering, Mentorship, Tithing

Chapter Topics:

Deciding on the Right Covering • What Is a Covering? • Determining Your Best Covering • The Need for Mentorship • Considerations for a Covering Relationship • Forming Covering Unions • Choosing Influence Rather Than Control • Motivations for Spiritual Covering • Lesser Better, Stronger Weaker Questions • Guidelines for Spiritual Coverers

T his section address three important practices of contemporary ministry, spiritual covering, mentorship, and tithing. It gives a quick look at the practical elements of ministry that affect all who enter God's service, regardless of their position. Everyone answering the call to serve the Lord will be concerned with a covering, that is relationships and connections that balance their teachings, aid in difficult times, and provide general ministry advice. They will also be concerned with mentorship, where veteran ministers guide and instruct new comers especially on the particulars of serving the Lord, dealing with His people, and navigating the church world. These people cross our ministry paths at different times for numerous purposes. However, the result is the same: they are there as part of the very critical hedge of defense that protects, informs, counsels and in some cases provides for junior ministers' success.

Often, the covering and the mentor are the same person, although that does not always have to be the case. Mentors serve distinctly different purposes in our lives that may equate to a covering, or simply serve as a tutor. And then there is the economic piece of the arrangement. How is a veteran minister to be compensated for his or her wisdom, experience, skill, and prominence in a junior's life? Traditionally, the means has been by the tithe or by paying dues. This subject is explored at length later in the chapter. Here we begin with the covering, and from there mentorship.

Deciding on the Right Covering

In the wake of prolific teaching on spiritual authority and the need for everyone in the Body of Christ to submit to it in the form of some type of ecclesiastical covering, ministers of all kinds are feverishly looking for their spiritual covering. They spend money on meetings, conferences, and classes trying to determine who should be their spiritual covering. Most of them are looking for what they have been taught is the ideal covering: someone they can trust, look up to, and most importantly, obey and follow. Obedience and service seem to feature most prominently in the requirements of a spiritual covering, but tend to, in most cases, emphasize the *coveree* more than the *covered*.

Frequently, covering seekers are told only what they must do—how they must comply—and all they need to bring to the relationship. Often there is little talk about what they, the *coveree*, will get from the arrangement, even after they have jumped through hoops to meet all its requirements. Actually, their benefits are usually quite vague, so what they get from the spiritual covering and the role the covering is to fill in their life and ministry are assumed. Questions that arise regarding spiritual covering concern the type of covering one should choose. Where should one look for his or her spiritual covering? What commitments should be made to one's spiritual covering, and what role should they fill? The answer to the latter question can be found by looking at the chart that follows. It shows a minimum of twelve actions the dedicated and conscientious covering should perform with those they take under their wing.

The Twelve Essential Roles of A Covering, Spiritual or Not

1.	Teacher	7.	Coach
2.	Promoter	8.	Collaborator
3.	Trainer	9.	Confidante
4.	Advisor	10.	Provider
5.	Mentor	11.	Influence
6.	Intercessor	12.	Authority

These may be viewed as the Twelve Roles of a Covering in general to be spiritually—more like ecclesiastically—applied in the church. The last two questions are quite pivotal. Look at this list, check off the things you seek in a governing, and draft a simple statement of how you wish to establish the relationship and what you are willing to give or forego for its success.

What Is a Covering?

From several sources, a covering addresses some concrete areas of the human and ministerial experience. It addresses teaching, protection, provision, closure, and opening. Look at the diagram below to see all that goes into a covering and later we will apply these to their spheres and realms of the church. Covering includes shielding, hiding when necessary, publishing and promoting. These elements should be discussed when covering conversations are initiated. These are all accomplished with continual contact, that is communication, correspondence, and interaction.

The Covering Tree

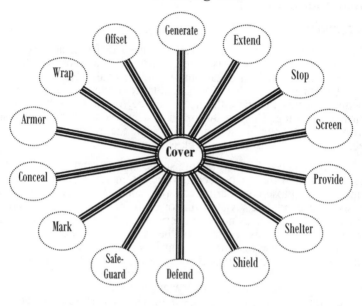

The next topic to address on this subject is how these are to be carried out under the heading of "spiritual." When the church begins to see the adjective spiritual being applied to itself as the ecclesia and the Holy Spirit, the answer becomes obvious. The Lord does all things by His Spirit and His Spirit ignites and confirms His word. Thus the answers to spiritual covering must conform to God's word and be submitted to the government of His Holy Spirit. You know them as the fruit of the Spirit, the law of the Spirit of Life in Christ Jesus, the manifestations of the Holy Spirit, and the grace gifts of the Spirit. The spirit of love, meekness, servitude, truth, honesty, loyalty and diligence are implied promises by those that choose to cover others in ministry. These are not set aside just because the nature of the relationship is narrowed to a veteran and a novice, or surrendered minister. Relationship principles do not vary according to their environments. The same practices that make for successful business, family, social, and filial relationships work just as well within the church, and really should work better and not worse. People know what reflects a good relationship and they expect to see the signs of it in their spiritual covering. Relationships are based on covenants and that means keeping one's word, being dutiful in one's responsibilities, and honoring the accepted norms of integrity all civilized peoples understand. Following these simple guidelines strengthens any covering arrangement, spiritual or otherwise.

Determining Your Best Covering

It is essential to determine what is needed from any type of professional or ministry based relationship. Sometimes people just want fellowship and an occasional sounding board. Here a network may be sufficient. Others want guidance collaboration on large ventures. In this instance, the need may be for an ally rather than a spiritual covering. Despite the belief that everyone needs a spiritual covering, that specific superior to relate and report to, it is not necessarily so, at least not in the classic sense.

Everyone needs friends, relationships, and accountability, but the degree to which they may need it varies from call to call. It is very important for those considering covering another to inquire about the prospective candidate's vision, history, life experience, and road to ministry. The Lord does not rear everyone up the same way nor does He put every minister through the same preparatory program. Therefore, it is wise to learn what made a minister what he or she is and how a covering can benefit or frustrate what the Lord has done and is doing in a life. Those seeking a covering must ascertain if it is an influence or authority that they want or need and at what juncture in their ministry journey they need it. The answer to this question decides the extent of involvement and submission to be covenanted.

People generally feel a call to more than one person as a covering. Some are drawn to one person's mantle, another's anointing, someone else's wisdom and counsel, another's teaching, training or mentorship; and still another's strength and leadership. If you look at the list you will see that one principle surfaces. Only one person in the group can be the authority figure in the spiritual covering spectrum. All the others are influencers in some capacity or other. They are of necessity *influencers* because what they provide does not require any more obedience and submission than what is needed to benefit from their short term or incidental involvement in a minister's life.

A mantle attraction or affinity may be intermittent, active only when the services of particular class of ministry is sought or rendered. The same is true for the anointing; its settings and impartations are situation driven. Wisdom is based on the need for counsel and likewise training and mentorship; when the class is over or the coaching complete the need for that type of ministry subsides, and the influence wanes. These interactions or encounters may sway decisions, affect actions, and even give some direction for a time, but what they lack is the governing aspect of authority that provokes ongoing obedience. For any number of reasons, their mantle fails to inspire a consistent surrender from the coveree, though what is said is heard and respected. Perhaps those ministers that do not garner a particular coveree's regard and favor sufficiently enough to guide and govern them are better suited for the Tutorial Arrangement, where the emphasis is not on authority but on knowledge.

A tutor differs from a covering in that he or she is limited to whatever facilitates the impartation of wisdom and the dispensing of knowledge and skill. Thus, a Tutorial Mentorship is likely to center on the veteran or senior minister sharing thoughts and imparting ideas the coveree merely gathers and stores. Natural friendship or at the least socialization may occur, but overall the relationship does not go beyond the respectful and mainly affective.

The word *tutor* is a late thirteenth century term that originally referred to a guardian, and began with the guardian angels assigned to a particular life. These were felt to mark certain highly skilled people to prepare a youngster or novice of his or her calling. Hence, the term "tutelary spirit." Since then the word has come to mean a private teacher on the order of a watcher. The tutor is a sage counsel and astute professional that seeks to ready the exceptionally gifted or especially talented for some future, usually lucrative career.

The purpose of a tutor in a life is to watch (in all prudent and practical contexts) over a promising person to equip him or her with what is needed to guarantee destiny and thereby steer it down its most prodigious course. The tutor as a watcher and handler of sorts takes the responsibility of vigilantly overseeing the anointed, very serious protégé. They are typically possessive in their guardianship, determined to ward off the distractions and deviations that can subvert a promising call. Tutors are usually quite confident in their abilities and dislike having their labors or time wasted. They know what aborts a destiny and tend to be overwhelmingly zealous about their charges to prevent it.

As you can see, tutoring, though less demanding than covering, is a big undertaking that has been too long trivialized by the church. Its tutors and tutelages have too long misunderstood its scope and thus sabotaged its function. The outcome has been frustrated tutors or mentors and embittered charges that felt their time and contributions were not well rewarded. Often we hear ministers that have sat under this one or that one, or submitted to this minister or that minister sometimes for decades, come away from the experience feeling cheated, and no closer to fulfilling their destiny than at the first.

Many things can account for this outcome, but the main one is usually misunderstanding and poor design of the arrangement at the outset. Next is a glimpse of what a tutorial looks like:

The Tutorial Cycle

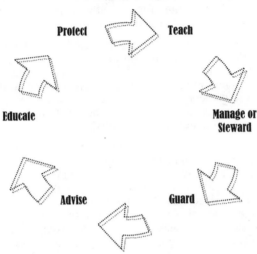

From the two diagrams shown, ministers should be careful about how they invite someone to cover them, and those that cover should be thoughtful about whom they choose to cover. There should be extensive discussion and thorough investigation to confirm that all parties to the agreement benefit. Perhaps a stipulated probationary period should be suggested to allow both sides to sever the relationship without hard feelings and undue costs should it not work out.

The Need for Mentorship

Tutoring is mentorship upgraded to the agency level. Here is where the mentor acts on behalf of the mentoree and doubles as an agent along with some of the features of the tutor, though not all may ever be experienced in a mentorship. The mentor knows he or she is taking on the task of securing a person's career potential and future success. Mentoring implies that the mentor sponsor the protégé's vocation, and present him or her to the world at the pre-appointed time. Mentoring, then, is time sensitive and goal-oriented.

Mentors intend to reap more than accolades or the gratification of knowing that they have released another excellent achiever into the world. They expect remuneration, as do the tutor, and acknowledgement. Mentors expect to be recognized as the source of the achiever's excellence. They want to be commemorated for their contribution to their progeny's style, skill, wisdom, and spirit and they want it more than casually. They want to be thanked, they want referrals, and they expect their protégés to keep them well supplied with next generation wonders to prepare for their fields throughout their professional careers.

Considerations for a Covering Relationship

An approximately eleventh century term as it has come down to us today, covering initially meant to close up[6]. When something covered, it is protected, furnished, and handled or implemented. These meanings should be a factor in any discussions on the subject. When the word is used, its many meanings should be explored to determine what one aims to receive and give in a covering arrangement.

Forming Covering Unions

Personality, viewpoints, and beliefs should be frankly discussed before any commitments are made. Limits of authority and commitment should be established with some type of loose scheduling agreed upon to reduce any overwhelming demands that can overtax either party to the union. A designated review period should be set to determine the success of the arrangement and identify ineffective areas and activities. At this frankly honest session, what is working well should be recognized and applauded and what needs help or elimination should be voiced without tension or offense. The boundaries of authority and influence should be set so that the accountability and responsibility elements of the covering are defined.

Those who take on a spiritual covering should benefit from the arrangement commensurate with the one providing the covering. It should not be a one-sided arrangement and compatibility issues should be strongly considered. Spiritual covering where the one covered is incompatible with the one chosen to do the covering or where there an imbalance exists between the two that causes friction should be averted. Coverees should not enter the arrangement with a sense of foreboding that everything they ever did or learned to date is disliked by the coverer. The coveree should not feel that every encounter is a corrective session with little or no encouragement or development. The smoldering resentment or unavoidable antipathy likely to result from such an environment can ruin the relationship, as hurt feelings impede its potential effectiveness.

Moreover, instances of envy, jealousy, and competition can fester and color discussions, motivating unfair treatment, and expose

---

[6] Dictionary of Etymology, Robert K. Barnhart

everyone concerned to unintentional hurt. If such emotions exist on the part of the authority figure, much damage can be done to the submitted minister. If it is the other way around, the subordinate minister the coverer hoped to benefit can defame the authority figure.

Choosing Influence Rather Than Control

Often ministers, in their eagerness to comply with the Lord's governmental system and means of regulating and protecting His ministries, jump headlong into covering relationships without giving them enough forethought. Simply because they want to be accepted and provided an outlet for their ministries, too many people find themselves bound to spiritual coverings that conflict with their callings or clash with their mantles. The cause of the situation is not taking time to determine what was intended by their spiritual covering, and what each expected from it or is willing to contribute to it.

Motivations for Spiritual Covering

Mostly, when people say they want a spiritual covering, what they really mean is they desire a dedicated counselor, advisor, door opener, or ministerial backer. Few are willing to alter their lives and surrender their liberty enough to earn or benefit from such desires. Not wrong in themselves, these desires can misrepresent the goal of a potentially good spiritual covering or frustrate it altogether.

On the other hand, coverers can themselves play the numbers game and rack up *coverees* as a gunslinger notches his gun. Here is a very futile reason to adopt sons and daughters as it is called. If the intent is to prove the coverer's influence and prestige, then it will be no more successful than a man impregnating many women to verify his virility. It does not make him a father, just an inseminator, and any test tube can do that these days. Parenting involves nurturing, and truthfully, not everyone is cut out to nurture. More than a few leaders have discovered their expansive charisma falls short of what it takes to be there for an up and coming minister, or to suckle a new church adequately enough for its survival. Most are that hyper-hormonal inseminator that just wants to see how many seeds he can spawn for the sake of virility.

The works these ministers birth (male or female) tend to struggle, falter, and succumb to a host of error and demonic activity in the same way a natural child is susceptible to similar onslaughts without proper parental covering. People who do not like people should not cover. Poor leaders, nurturers, and communicators should not cover. Leaders that do not like answering questions, dealing with wounded emotions and broken souls should not cover, nor should those that dread being

154

in crowds, hate being imposed upon or interrupted. Those that resent having to be on call, obliged to receive others indiscriminately, or being available, should not cover. These are examples of poor attitudes upon which to handle another's trust. Coverers are so by covenant. They pledge to occupy the stead of all those areas stated in the Covering Tree, and taking people's funds and not doing so is fraudulent. Identifying a covering is risky in itself; submitting to one that just cannot fulfill the terms and implications of the arrangement is detrimental and should be avoided.

When testing the waters for a covering, seriously explore motives. There are those that see the need for authority figures over their ministries, and sometimes over their lives. Such people are drawn to extremely charismatic leaders, especially if they are prominent or strong, dominating ministers who tend to take control of their charges' lives. In these cases, an indolent minister can risk being told what to do, how to do it, when and what to minister and when and what not to minister. Submitting to strong authority figures can be positive if the one submitting is of a strong character and focused outlook, otherwise such an arrangement can be devastating.

Negatively, the control figure becomes the lone commander and chief over weaker ministers because that is the sole reason the pact exists. There is little thought of training, development, skills building, or inner personal enrichment. The commander speaks rules, and the subordinate listens and obeys. Again, if one feels the need to cast all their care onto an elder minister to feel validated for ministerial service, it is no crime. Once more, such an arrangement is not inherently wrong in and of itself. However, over time, an overbearing covering will ultimately spoil the relationship and the future ministry of the subordinate.

What needs to be explored by the one seeking spiritual covering is the reason they see a spiritual covering is necessary in the first place: Why should they be covered by anyone at all, and what type of covering is best for them? Some people, for instance, have pastoral covering because a strong pastor is sufficient. However, apostles, for instance, tend to outpace their shepherds spiritually once they are awakened to the office, and that can be unsettling as the apostle's insight and range of spirituality can overwhelm the pastors. Tensions under these circumstances easily build, so they have to separate.

Stronger ministers need stronger coverings, but even under these conditions, the terms of the accord should be thoroughly discussed. Many factors go into forming the covering arrangement. Unfortunately, most are ignored until a crisis forces their handling. Wise spiritual covering arrangements are better served by anticipating the likely disruptions or conflicts that invariably crop up in any kind of alliance, collaboration, or spiritual union. Below are some issues or questions that could be addressed:

- Why should the arrangement be established in the first place?

- Is the lesser in the agreement really to be blessed by the better and is it clear who is the lesser and who is the better?

- If the subordinate has more to offer, will the tables turn and the *coverer* become the subordinate?

- Is the ideal arrangement to be based upon influence or authority?

- Is it to be a professional alliance or a parental connection?

- What are the limits of authority and control and who decides them?

- Are decisions to be joint ventures or does the *coverer* retain all control?

- What happens as the subordinate grows? If he or she increases in stature, how does that affect the initial arrangement? Should it continue as is, be modified or resolved, and how?

- Who evaluates the subordinate's growth and by what standards and criteria is it done?

As you can see, the questions and matters concerning spiritual covering are extensive. It is rare that those embarking upon such alliances thoroughly investigate seriously the aspects and potentials that lie ahead of them. Far too often, the covering arrangement is based upon spiritual enthusiasm, flattery, or emotional zeal, which cannot withstand the inevitable onslaughts all relationships face.

Lesser Better, Stronger Weaker Questions

Previously, the phrase "lesser and better" was used to call into question the viability of certain covering arrangements and those considering them. It is common for newcomers and unknowns to seek covering from forerunners and renowned ministers for a myriad of prudent and self-serving reasons.

If the newcomer is not a novice but merely an unknown, or even more threatening, an up and coming catalyst for what the Lord will do next, the outcome of such a covering relationship can be disturbing as the Saul-David Syndrome kicks in. Here is where the incumbent

156

authority figure recognizes the Lord's intentions in his or her subordinate and fears the inevitable effects of having brought the newcomer into his or her sphere of ministry.

This crushingly painful scenario is all too frequent and hardly anyone rising from the ranks of the unknown escapes it. Although it is impossible to avoid completely since our Savior endured such hostility, it is possible to foresee and avert its constant repetition. Here are a few clues to the possible pitfalls of an unhealthy or imbalanced spiritual covering relationship. Ask the following:

1. Is a proposed mentor, parent in the Lord, or spiritual covering on par experientially, intellectually, or emotionally?

2. Has the *coveree* achieved more spiritually, practically, or ministerially in their short time in the Lord than the one considered for covering?

3. Does newcomer brightness and keenness bother the spiritual covering?

Be alert to unfounded criticism, abrupt dismissals, or refusals to allow contributions to covering minister's world. How ministers share their heart, handle what newcomers or enamored subordinates submit can frustrate an intimate and long-term relationship.

Grooming for successful and effective ministry requiring seeking God less and regarding or listening to the people more, or suggestions to gather messages from extra biblical sources rather than the Holy Spirit, from the mentor covering could veer genuine ministers away from their first love and Christ's foundation in ministry. Such circumstances will not reward for God's truth but rather be shunned and rejected because of it.

Guidelines for Spiritual Coverers

No fruitful relationship can endure one-sidedness. Just as the person seeking a covering must examine his or her motives, so must those who feel called to cover others. It is not enough to care about or admire an up and coming or dynamic minister. Questions concerning the need to commit to another in ministry and take responsibility for him or her should be honestly answered. Here are a few to start with:

1. Why bother to assume responsibility for another?

2. What would you give to such a relationship and what do you expect to receive in return?

3. What type of people do you work best with and what type of people are you least effective?

157

4. Do I have a successful enough record of accomplishment with empowering people for ministry to cover anyone else?

5. Am I good and yet inoffensive, at confrontation, evaluations, and objectivity?

6. Am I to cover as a parent, a coach, a mentor, or a trainer?

7. Am I expected to provide ministry outlets, to open doors otherwise closed to those I cover?

8. Honestly speaking, am I looking to develop people or to be served?

9. How are my interpersonal and people-building skills?

10. What developmental resources do I have on hand or at my disposal to develop others?

11. What am I prepared to impart to others as a spiritual covering?

12. How much authority should I require from the relationship?

Of course there is more, but you do get the point. Furthermore, it is understood that matters of integrity, criminality, addictions and abuses, and reputation are to be discovered by all concerned. Due diligence should not be shirked. Anyone convinced they need a spiritual covering or should be one ought to take steps to understand why and how such a one can benefit, protect, and guide another's ministry.

The type of covering settled on should be clearly defined, established as envisioned by both parties, and not unduly stressful to either one. If it is to be one of influence, then a network not interested in telling ministers what to do or assuming control of their ministries may be enough. Should authority figures be needed to entrust one's leadership and government to, then an association network will be insufficient. A spiritual parent, direct leader, or outright superior is a better choice. The decision to enter all alliances and the relationships that affect ability to hear and obey the Lord must be made with eyes wide open.

CHAPTER TWELVE

Spiritual Covering & Tithing

Chapter Topics:

What's a Tithe? • The Rightful Recipient of the Tithe • The Melchizedek Tithe • Understanding the Ancient Temple • Spiritual Covering & the Tithe

---

O
f late, there is much debate and consternation over the matter of tithing. When it comes to spiritual coverings, the matter is intense. Those that have submitted to a covering are irritated by the demand to tithe to that covering for what is presumably spiritual services, many of which have yet to be explained. Previously, we have discussed spiritual covering from the perspective of a mentor, a tutor, an authority, and an influence. Just think for a moment of the demand all those different spiritual benefactions put on a tithe. Does one tithe to the covering as a mentor, tutor, advisor, or as a promoter? Do they tithe to the influencer or the authority? Who makes the decision and what is it based upon?

Here, to wrap up the discussions, the matter of how to handle the tithe as a leader and to whom those in authority tithe is addressed. To do so, let us begin at the beginning by answering first what the tithe is, how it began, and its founding premise. Often when people can follow the line of thinking on a matter, they can arrive at sound conclusions concerning its policies, practices, and revelations. That is what this chapter will do. First, what is the tithe?

Literally, tens of thousands of dollars are given to spiritual coverings worldwide and precious few of the tithers can say what they got for their money, and the tithe is money. Since it is money, the question invariably arises, what does one get in return for his or her tithe to his or her spiritual covering? The number one foundation of the tithe is that it is a war tax. That is how it came to God's people in the first place.

History of the Tithe?

Abraham, having won the war between himself and the five kings, as a thank offering to the Almighty who wrought his victory, rendered a tenth of his spoils to the Lord's lone priesthood on earth. Melchizedek met Abraham returning from his unbelievable slaughter and administered his first communion with his new God. Abraham's history as a Babylonian prophet no doubt educated him on divine protocol; for example, one always gives the first fruit of the war spoils to the god responsible for one's victory.

Perhaps Abraham knew Melchizedek or he appeared in what was commonly accepted as priestly garments for his day. Either way, Israel's progenitor knew that the Almighty gave him his victory and was entitled to its war tax, also called back then a death tax. [7] The normal war tax for most kings, according to several sources, was one fifth. The other fifth went to the generals that won the battle. Abraham in effect gave the Lord a double portion as it appears he gave his warrior's portion to the Lord as well. Melchizedek in turn blessed Abraham and ratified the Lord's covenant with the man that would found His only portion of the human race. The Most High's priest added Abraham's spoils to the treasury to continue to have meat in the Lord's storehouse for the priests under his care and the priestly village Melchizedek founded and maintained, which brings us to our next point.

The Rightful Recipient of the Tithe

The tithe goes to the priest of the temple to maintain it, pay its workers, and provide for its replenishment. Back in Abraham's time, the temple was the same as the village as most deities' temples were

---

[7] Roget's International Thesaurus, St. Martins Press, 1965

160

situated in the center of the village surrounded by the rest of its community. To be over the temple was to be over the region that housed it. That is how powerful priests were back then. They represented the highest level of government and anointed every other official beneath them. What makes this important is the reason the Lord appointed the tithe in the first place and why it ends with the priest of the house.

Most people are familiar with the concept of a priest. They know that they are ministers ordained to officiate for their gods. The epistle to the Hebrews, chapters seven through nine, gives an abbreviated explanation of priests, their minimal functions, and obligations to their gods and their people. It is a course version of the Law, Moses, and the Levitical Priesthood. Priests are ordinarily stationed at their temple sites whether that is in the temple or about its precincts. They receive offerings and sacrifices, slaughter and prepare them for presentation to the god of the land; train worshippers in divine service and how to correctly approach, and appease, the god of the land. The priests teach the gods' laws and statutes, history and testimony. They also prepare other priests to succeed them.

In the book of Leviticus, the priests also diagnosed sicknesses and diseases, identified mold in the home, exposed adulterous wives, and mediated and governed in the name of the deity. The priests inquired of the god, interpreted divine response, and supervised the temple workers and its possessions. They overall administrated its daily affairs. Succinctly speaking, this is the gist of the priest's work and he or she is usually compensated for such expansive services from the tithes and offerings presented. This is what Malachi 3:10 is addressing when it says the Lord's house must have meat in its storehouse.

The Melchizedek Tithe

One ongoing debate raging in the church is the validity of tithes under the New Testament. The argument is that the Lord did away with the reason for the tithe when He concluded the Old Testament and Moses' Law. It would be valid if the tithe began with Moses, which it did not.

The Bible introduces the tithe in Genesis 14:20 where Abraham gave Melchizedek, not Moses, a tithe of all he won in slaughtering the five kings. Peculiarly, the tithe, like faith, predates Moses and the Law. They began as part of Abraham's covenant into which the children of Israel were born. That means it is by faith and not according to the Law of Moses that tithes were paid. Faith is what ascribed God's righteousness to Abraham, making the tithe a spiritual act of faith.

161

The priest that administrated the first tithes to be paid on earth to the Most High is Melchizedek and not Aaron. Melchizedek is an eternal being. Hebrews chapter seven says that he is without father or mother, beginning of days or end of life. That makes him eternal (in our sense) and immortal. Hence, the first priest to receive the Lord's tithe was not human or earthly. He was sent from heaven by the Creator to lay the foundation for the birth of His first nation, Israel. Melchizedek is the priest of eternity and not earth. His priesthood paved the way for the Lord Jesus' installation as High Priest according to the order of Melchizedek. Hebrews calls the Lord's first priesthood unending and unchanging. Jesus took over as High Priest of an eternal priesthood that subsists on the power of an endless life.

What do all these facts about Melchizedek tell us but that tithing is an eternal and heavenly custom given as a gift to humanity? It assures God's vital transactions between heaven and earth are unimpeded. Those who base the tithe and its cessation on Moses fail to trace its origins back far enough. If Jesus is the High Priest of eternity according to the order of Melchizedek who founded his priesthood on earth before Jerusalem was Salem and before the Jebusites took over the area, then two things become evident. The tithe and faith are both eternal and that means without end.

The New Testament church may not have to pay tithes according to the Moses' Levitical Priesthood as sinners kept for redemption, but it should pay tithes to the Lord Jesus Christ based on Melchizedek's priesthood, to whom Abraham, the father of our faith, paid it. That is the gist of what Psalm 110:4 prophesies and Hebrews chapter seven says Christ accomplished. Study the chapter and pay close attention to verse eight: "*And here men that die receive tithes; but there he receiveth them, of whom it is witnessed that he liveth.*" Tithes today go to Jesus and not Aaron, nor on the basis of the Levitical order. For this, if for no other reason than the Holy Spirit filled the Christian with the Godhead, passing them from death to life and from Satan's power to God's that the saint should desire to finance the Lord's kingdom on earth.

Of the nine times the word *tithes* is used in the New Testament, six of them are in the book of Hebrews and they are all about Melchizedek, the eternal priest. Each time the Almighty declares Jesus' priesthood, He always decrees it is forever. Therefore, if Melchizedek's priesthood came before Aaron and Jesus entered it as its High Priest, then Melchizedek and his priests were alive and well at the time of His resurrection and ascension. This eternal priesthood is apparently the one that received the spirit of all those animals Aaron's order offered up to the Almighty for centuries, confirming the

162

principle that everything earthly has a spiritual prototype upon which it subsists.

As a result of this revelation, the argument about tithes in the New Testament church is unfounded. The church is an eternal entity stationed on earth. When its natural founder paid the first tithes, it was to the eternal and heavenly priesthood that he paid them. Here is what Hebrews 7:9-11 means: *"And as I may so say, Levi also, who receiveth tithes, payed tithes in Abraham. For he was yet in the loins of his father, when Melchisedec met him. If therefore perfection were by the Levitical priesthood, (for under it the people received the law,) what further need was there that another priest should rise after the order of Melchisedec, and not be called after the order of Aaron?"*

Understanding the Ancient Temple

Ancient temple precincts housed livestock, granaries, agriculture, beverages for the libations, war spoils, an arsenal, and a precious metals and gemstone vault, if it belonged to a famous and victorious deity. These storages were huge and maintaining them all employed extensive personnel beside the priests and ministers. From accounting to inventory, from collections to distribution, from security to supervision, the temple areas of the ancient world were busy industrial centers. They supplied the community, defended and horded the god's treasuries and wealth, and financed its people's existence. What all this seemingly unrelated information shows is the importance of the tithe.

The accumulated tithe was intended to cover the living expenses of every member of the community. It provided the economy of the commonwealth, and the priest's sustenance for serving in the temple. Administrating it was part of their other extensive duties; how they earned their living. When the church was born, the priests that received the hordes of the Lord were replaced by the apostles and that is the point of this discussion.

The apostles' early collections reminisced the extraordinary giving in the ancient temples. In addition, their purposes for receiving the bounty were the same as the priests: to distribute to the church at large, so that none among them lacked or had any need (read Acts 4:32, 37). Moreover, the ancient Levites were replaced by the seven deacons chosen to do for the church what the Levites did for ancient Israel (Acts 6:3, 4). This is because the twelve tribes are enfolded in the New Creation. Paul teaches us in 1 Corinthians 2:13 to compare spiritual things with spiritual. In relation to spiritual coverings and the tithes, coverers need to occupy the seat of the priest of the house and completely perform its functions to earn it.

As for tithing, one wonders where scripture says the tithe of Israel made a national circuit. Where are we told that the northern temple precinct tithed to the south and the south the north and the north the west and the west the east? Would it not be redundant for them to do so if the tithed ended up where it began? While this was being done, how were the needs of the people handled and who administrated this circuit?

Today's ministers demanding the tithe because of being the seasoned or senior minister is questionable at best. What do they do with the tithe that even remotely resembles what the ancient Bible pattern portrays? How is the tithe of the coveree stored and for whose benefit? How is an accounting made and under what guidelines do today's recipients of the tithe perform 2 Corinthians 12:14? *"Behold, the third time I am ready to come to you; and I will not be burdensome to you: for I seek not yours, but you: for **the children ought not** to lay up for the parents, **but the parents for the children."***

Somehow, according to this wisdom, tithes received by coverers should be lay something for the coverees as a hedge against possible disaster in the future. The tithe is not only a war tax, but it is also a retainer that assures God's intervention when and if calamity comes, if we are to use the Lord's handling of His tithes as a model. Tithes are a type of insurance payment that stores (lays up) claim money or resources in advance of crises. Lastly, the tithe is a guard that prevents encroaching terrorists from invading a saint's safety to wreak havoc at will.

Spiritual Covering & the Tithe

If all these requirements are true for those that receive today's tithes, then much more should be expected and given in return. Coverers are going to have to deliver more in exchange for the tithe they take in the name of a priest or its equivalent. Those that tithe to them should legitimately anticipate some hedge against disaster and hardship should it happen down the line. They should expect to be counseled, coached, mentored, advanced, and promoted because that is what secular counterparts to Christian ministry assure their supporters. Integrious leaders would never presume to take anyone's funds under false pretenses, coercion, or without giving them something of equal or greater value in return. Doing so on the ground of a purely ethereal return can appear to be a type of spiritual exploitation.

If your coverer requires the tithe, he or she will need to provide what the early church and ancient Israel provided for it. There should be discounts, rebates, savings, low interest loans, or something concrete in exchange, especially when the tither falls on hard times. The coverer should perform the same or equivalent priestly functions as those from whom they took their pattern. It is a risky practice to divert the tithe from the temple and its needs to one's personal interests. Hording that tithe for personal gain and not laying up some of it for the tither to fulfill the whole word of God is dangerous.

It may be better for coverers to assess a duty or fee to their service. Perhaps charging tuition for tutoring, counseling fees for mentorship, and specific retainers for eventual services is more appropriate. A more sensible approach could be to assess a single monthly amount comparable to what the coverer performs in the arrangement.

CHAPTER THIRTEEN

Responsible Protocols for Spiritual Coverings

Chapter Topics:

A Biblical Model for Spiritual Coverings • Quality Spiritual Covering Protocols • Staffing Protocols • Tithing Protocols

The term *spiritual covering* does not mean heavenly or celestial, nor utterly out of the range of the definitive. The church under the Holy Spirit regulated by God's word defines spiritual covering. It simply means ecclesiastical, Spirit filled and led, logos and rhema balanced. Spiritual coverers should avoid impressing ethereal motives upon their coverees that exempt them from attaching tangible values to their protection. Christian coverers' values should exceed prayers and extend to a concrete exchange of ministry services for funds received that at least somewhat mirrors what ancient tithes provided.

Christ's apostles that received the membership's wealth laid at their feet provided the early church with tangible and intangible benefits of their apostleship. They saw to it that there was no lack among any of them from what was laid at their feet. It should not be that a network with faithful tithers has no means of receiving help as supporters of a particular ministry in times of crises, even if that aid is only a referral databank of community agencies that can do so. It should provide some relief. Leviticus 27:30 makes it plain that the tithe is the Lord's.

It is His because whatever one acquires from his or her labors was made by Him. All that qualifies as a tithe is composed of what God made and possesses. It comes from God. That is the reason why it is inherently His. While there is no question that a laborer is worthy of his (or her) from the lowest of tithes, wages as the Lord says, the church needs to be sure that wages are not what is owed one's spiritual covering rather than the tithe. If the title is due one's covering, they should provide, even if only minimally at first, the full range of services typically performed by priests.

A Biblical Model for Spiritual Coverings

A responsible model for spiritual coverings' duty to earn their tithe is no different from what the church was built upon. The Bible is explicit about how to receive and process, store, accumulate, and distribute the tithe. Coverers themselves need to have stationed headquarters with reliable communications systems to receive and respond to calls and correspondence from those they cover. There should be a personnel staff to meet, greet, and serve those that commit to the ministry. Those that tithe to them should insist on it. The inexcusable attitude of today's great ministers that they have no obligation to their supporters and tithers, because they are too busy getting more to ignore, is unfortunate and borderline abusive. It confirms the sinner's negative opinion of the church because its leaders do not subscribe to the same professional protocols they are obliged to in secular businesses. After all, as we like to say in ministry circles, the church is a business and if this is true, it should act like one.

Quality Spiritual Covering Protocols

A good spiritual covering protocol resembles this: A contact begets at contact, colleagues and peers personally return calls to colleagues whenever possible, assistants respond to other assistants, and contacts to all others are made by lower staff. Everyone that reaches out to a ministry they have supported in any way should receive a return communication in some format that shows interest in them and the intent to address their concern. Promises should be kept in a timely matter and gratitude expressed for loyalty. Orders and requests should be processed promptly and shipped expediently. Errors should be frankly admitted and reversed speedily. Promised compensation for losses and missed dates should be quickly remediated.

Criticism, problems, and complaints should generally merit even cursory investigation and receive explanatory responses as a matter of courtesy. Christian leaders must become as bold and adept at handling the pleasant and unpleasant tasks and events associated with their vocations as they are about souls, opportunities, and contacts. Staff members should be well trained in customer service, courteous and diligent. Supervisors should regularly review the procedures and correct deficiencies. When people deal with ministers, they ought to feel they are being served by the Lord and every effort should be made to avoid misrepresenting Him and disillusioning them. These are some minimal integrity protocols that all those entrusted in public service, ministry or not, should implement and observe.

Staffing Protocols

In addition, coverers should be full time staff, such as what ancient priests had, to take calls, make callbacks, and schedule meetings. They should receive discounts on products, not necessarily free, and be honored for keeping the coverer's ministry thriving. The most successful coverers should have prayer teams on hand to take prayer requests and counselors to handle the problems their tithers encounter in the course of ministry life. These could be assigned to subordinate ministers the coverer has engaged with part of the tithe money received from those they cover. Coverers should accumulate resource tools to offer their tithers and supporters on a variety of topics, themes, and issues and have a means for them to access or acquire them for ministry. There should be designated recognition, reward, and award protocols in place to distinguish those that tithe as supporters from the others the coverer relates to in ministry. The tithers should get something for their money, starting with special attention and preferential treatment among the masses that just follow the ministry and 'bless' it from time to time.

All these benefits the Lord gives His church for their tithes. Besides them, He gives them preferential treatment and elevated status among His other spiritual hosts, and releases exceptional favor in the realms of men. God opens doors, rescues, enhances productivity, enriches, and blesses their land. He teaches, guides, counsels, heals, intercedes and intervenes for, replenishes, and unifies His people. He fellowships and communes with them, tending to their sorrows, averting their crises, and overturning their calamities. The Lord uses His reputation to influence their lives, prosper their endeavors, and return what was stolen or lost, sending help and provisions in times of need as well. These He does because He has vowed to do so as He promised because of the tithe.

Tithing Protocols

It is incumbent upon God to earn the advances paid for His later and ongoing intervention in life's unexpected crises that are secured by the tithes regularly paid to Him. God's is an institution, an organization that, like the ancient temple precincts, provides a multitude of essential and intermittent services to His creation. These are compounded when delivered to His ecclesia. As due remuneration for His services and a hedge against disaster, deprivation, or disease, He ordained the tithe. God's kingdom is tantamount to a nation with the duties and responsibilities of a government.

The tithe is a war tax and citizen tribute. Consequently, one would hardly think of giving one's taxes to anyone other than the government's official authorities appointed to receive and distribute them so that it performs its word to its citizenry. Moreover, citizens would hardly continue paying taxes to a government that gave them nothing for it in return. This is just basic monetary reasoning. It should never be that anyone who tithed faithfully to a ministry or minister for years that undergoes a crisis receives nothing from that ministry in times of trouble. They should not be told to tithe and not receive the same advantage and leverage the Lord gives not only immaterially but materially as well. Those that take their tithe should use their influence and authority to intervene on the tithers's behalf and pull from the resources years of tithes help build to aid those that have been supporting, even if it is with contacts, referral and referral services, counsel, guides, wisdom and the word of the Lord. That calls for a staff, an agency of services, and an inventory of goods and products to be accumulated from what is taken. Tithers to spiritual coverings should never receive for their faithfulness a wall of silence. That is not why the Lord entrusts His tithe in any leader's hands. He expects them to respond with His response systems and be there for His people in His stead as He would be if He were physically present. It is why the Lord thought to prosper certain skillful and administratively talented people in the first place.

CHAPTER FOURTEEN
Mentorship

Chapter Topics:

Traditional Mentorship Formation • Indicators of a Promising Mentorship • Critical Requirements of Suitable Mentors • Indicators of an Unstable Mentorship Mix • Mentoree Duties: Coming under Your Mentor's Wing

No comprehensive treatment of this subject would be complete without a discussion on mentoring. Mentorship is an official function where a seasoned, well connected veteran of the field takes a novice or junior under his or her wing. Spiritually speaking, mentorship is a joint agreement where one who is called to a specific sphere of God's service seeks and surrenders to a like-minded senior in their calling to learn the ins and outs of the office.

Mentorship may or may not include tutoring, but it always involves coaching, counseling, guidance, and practice. What is scarcely known is that mentorship is supposed to provide skill outlets and professional opportunities. Otherwise, why would a junior or novice submit his or her life and liberty to another's care? Here is where the conflict begins because both parties to the arrangement must agree on its purposes, goals, and objectives. They must together identify and employ the methods, requirements, and the standards by which their mentorship is measured.

Mentorship must be distinguished from attendance where a servant attaches himself or herself to a seasoned professional for the specific purposes of attending to their private affairs and personal needs. In this instance, the primary goal is to see to their comfort. That is, unfortunately, how many Christian mentorships are conducted as overworked and overwhelmed ministers assign their menial tasks and personal needs to an eager soul yearning to be used of God. Frequently, in these types of arrangements, the server may or may not understand that the developmental and opportunity aspects of the mentorship secretly hoped for will not happen.

To avoid the confusion, and omit the frustration and anguish such situations can breed, a candid understanding of the nature of a servanthood relationship and its outcomes or benefits should be spelled out in advance. Those attending to prestigious ministers should be honest about their motives and the limits of their service. They should frankly disclose what they expect from their services, whether it is prayer, personal gratification, finances, opportunities, etc. The senior ministers should likewise be open and honest about what they need from an attendant and what they are willing to supply in return. If the minister is willing to be a mentor, not only should he or she say so, but also the terms and conditions under which the veteran is willing to lend his or her expertise to the junior's development should be specified.

Traditional Mentorship Formation

Ordinarily, mentors choose their mentorees and not the other way around. The child rarely chooses the parent and if so, it does not nullify the parent's obligation to the majority of the provision and training involved in the readiness process. The idea of a newcomer or unknown minister approaching a well known one to declare him or her to be the newcomer's mentor is common; however, it is not only awkward, but it is also inconsistent with the natural order of life. Juniors may easily latch on to their elders but they can not dictate the elder's response or agreement. A negative outcome of this practice is that the juniors who forged the mentorship on their personal grounds, tends to sever ties at their will when things do not go their way. Once the mentor takes the union seriously, the junior minister or novice can balk at its demands and structure and feel free to abandon the mentorship because it was their idea in the first place. Many times, this is how Christian mentorships are born. In some cases, the elder minister is approached, often at a very vulnerable time, and told by some eager young minister that God told them, "You are my mentor."

171

Expecting joy and confirmation, many of them walk away from the encounter confused when experienced ministers respond with caution and do not jump at the chance to obey their word from the Lord. In other cases, the tenderhearted elder minister just acquiesces to the declaration, unsure of how to tactfully get out of it. Generally, these two models are how Christian mentorships form and depending upon which of two birthed the arrangement, a healthy or extremely dysfunctional relationship begins.

A third scenario is where a weighed down minister realizes that he or she has grown to the point that personal assistance beyond the clerical and administrative is needed. This is the most difficult and vulnerable position in which overwhelmed ministers can be found since it exposes their intimate concerns to another they must rely on to handle their personal needs. Many people filling this role in a minister's life fail to comprehend the inner struggle most of them experience before entrusting their private selves to another's care. Such exposure can be helpful or detrimental and choosing the right person to handle the task is critical.

Often the overwhelmed minister waits, usually for the above reasons, until the situation is dire and is forced to hastily appoint someone out of sheer necessity. If the most available person has not been purged, groomed, and pruned by the Lord for the assignment, the results can be disastrous as a critical spirit mercilessly uncovers the elder minister, spreading private matters abroad. The converse of the situation is when the elder seeks to offload personal matters quickly and implies to a willing candidate that more will come out of the relationship than actually will. Here is where a dutiful servant diligently attends to the elder minister in the hope that he or she will be rewarded with promising ministry opportunities later. Such an arrangement can go on for years until the servant wakes up and realizes the implied promise is never going to happen. Feeling hurt and betrayed, the naïve attendant severs the arrangement seriously wounded.

Again, the outcome is tragic as a once potentially wonderful attendant is jaded and embittered at having been abused. This is called the "Ahab-Jacob Syndrome." We all know the story; Ahab promised Jacob something for his services for a specified period of time with no intention of honoring his word. He deceived Jacob until the young man, by God's providence, forced Ahab to perform his word. Many young attendants have been burned by the Ahab game and are quite cynical as a result, which is a prudent reason to probe mentorship opportunities carefully.

What all these examples share is their power to determine the success or failure of a mentorship. To avoid difficulties, everyone involved should be clear about the aims of the mentorship they want to form. Here are a few things to consider when deciding the hopes of your mentorship.

Indicators of a Promising Mentorship

A promising and fruitful mentorship should offer the following:

1. Protection from failure, faults, the unscrupulous and naiveté.

2. Preparation for God's eventual use or promotion.

3. Instillation of wisdom, insight, vocational knowledge, and protocol.

4. Perspective shaping that alters and conforms, previous views and errant expectations to the realities of the call.

5. Impartation of the spirit and sentiments of the call.

6. Practical skills building that reflect the demands and duties of the calling.

7. Agency support as the mentor reaches out to his or her constituency to pave the way for the mentoree's eventual entrance into the field.

To succeed the mentoree must be available, submissive, diligent, and teachable. Instructions must be followed, details completed, assignments and tasks carried out as instructed. Excuses and task evasion should be avoided, while open and honest behavior and conduct expectations should be defined and followed. If prescribing to the Bible's model, the mentor has the right to set schedules, make unusual demands, and do all possible to simulate the world of the calling the mentoree is aspiring to enter. Realism is the greatest tool of an effective mentorship as the mentor includes true reenactments of what the mentoree will face in the field as a regular part of the arrangement. Here is where novice mentors fail in the mentorship. A mentor on the rise cannot lift a mentoree above where he or she has not gone. The following are some other significant factors to take under advisement as you consider the best mentor for you.

Critical Requirements of Suitable Mentors

1. The mentor must admire and appreciate you as a person and a potential peer and colleague.

2. The mentor must be able to relate to your readiness journey and the experiences and processes you encountered along the way.

3. The mentor must appreciate and understand the wisdom and value of the life experiences that made you who you are.

4. The mentor must not envy you, who you are, and what you bring to the relationship. Here, the Hebrews 7 "lesser is blessed by the better" principle especially applies.

5. The mentor must not need what you have more than you need what they can deliver to get you where you are going.

6. The mentor must not view you as a rival and a contender for his or her fame and success.

7. The mentor must have an honest insight into the struggles and warfare you face being uniquely you pursuing your particular call.

8. The mentor must exceed you in knowledge, competence, wisdom, and exposure to the field.

9. The mentor must enjoy observing your present capabilities and delight in developing them further to ready you for God's service.

10. The mentor must enjoy hearing the details of your development process as you review what you have learned, and where and how you have improved under his or her hand.

In addition, it is helpful to recognize the signs of an unsuitable mentor. Unsuitable, in this case, means unsuitable for you, not necessarily unsuited to the call of mentorship. Human nature being what it is, relational chemistry is largely emotions driven. Sometimes for any number of reasons personalities and temperaments clash and that makes for a bad mentorship mix. Below are some points that can prove insightful to the mentor and the mentoree as they probe the feasibility of forming a mentorship together. A mentorship arrangement should be avoided if too many of the following indicators exist.

Indicators of an Unstable Mentorship Mix

1. The mentor starts out with a list of "fix you's" before identifying your strengths, learning your world or your life.

2. The mentorship is mainly built around the mentor, and ignores your development needs.

3. The mentor limits access to his or her expertise and assistance by being routinely unavailable.

4. The mentor makes definite demands but gives vague commitments.

5. Your servanthood is more important than your development.

6. Your labors are praised while your growth, skills, and development are ignored.

7. The mentor does not value your professional contribution to the relationship.

8. The mentor disdains your wisdom and advice.

9. Most sessions and encounters with the mentor center on criticism and correction.

10. Your strengths and weaknesses are inequitably recognized and treated.

11. The mentor relentlessly crucifies your natural ability, temperament, and personality, preferring to alter who you are and how you are made rather than cultivate your gifts and talents for the purpose which you were made.

12. The mentoring atmosphere seems to be constantly one of threat and disapproval.

13. The mentor readily receives your ideas and creations and uses them personally without giving you due credit as their creator.

14. The mentor regularly harvests your gifts and talents for personal gain by never giving you a platform to practice them or an audience to field test your growth.

15. The mentor refuses to acknowledge you in public.

16. The mentor refuses to give you the time and attention you request to grow, improve, and become competent in your calling.

17. The mentor consistently compares you with others and demeans you publicly under the guise of humbling you so you don't fall in the future.

18. The mentor does not seem to value your time, obligations, and need for his or her attention as demonstrated by ignoring calls, overlooking your presence in special sessions, and not ever choosing you to be part of a significant event or to fulfill a significant part in them, even after years.

19. You often leave your mentor's presence depressed, devalued, and frustrated rather than motivated.

20. The mentor responds to your experiments with criticism, achievements with disinterest, and your challenges with accusations or judgment.

21. The mentor shows little interest in you as a person outside of your service, gifts, and contributions exercised to him or her personally.

These are but a few of the behaviors you should consider and note as you give your mentorship the trial run and probationary period it needs to prove itself valuable to you and the mentor. Mentors ought to review them to detect nagging thoughts or resistance to mentorees that they cannot quite identify. It may be that you, the mentor, are not the one for the person in your life determined to make you take them under your wing. That constant irritation you vaguely wrestle with concerning them just may be God's way of saying this one is not for you to groom.

Mentoree Duties: Coming Under Your Mentor's Wing

Taken from my book *Church Prophets*, the following suggestions are made concerning yielding to a mentorship. At the least, be ready to comply with the following:

1. Be honest about your actions, reactions, motives, offenses, and defenses as you enter and interrelate in your mentorship.

2. Honestly, confront yourself and question your motives, truthfully appraising your real self in another's eyes.

3. Critique yourself in view of your required mentorship duties and your attitude toward them.

4. Face and explore your relational and service history, fears, doubts, anger, and resistance, particularly as they pertain to authority figures.

5. Ask yourself how selfishly motivated you may have been in establishing your mentorship and if you have a real problem committing to its development in any area connected to the mentorship that should be promptly handled.

6. Are you really interested in being successful in God, and what will you sacrifice for that success?

7. Will your pride, your ego, or your independence get in the way of your receiving from, serving and benefiting from your mentor's expertise?

8. What did you expect to get from, and give to and for, your present and future ministry success?

9. Are your expectations fantasy? If not, how realistic are they?

10. Now that you have given your word to be mentored by this person, are you going to back out of it or will you see it through to the end of what you know the Lord called you to do?

Though these are tough questions to answer, their necessity cannot be overstressed before entering a mentorship. When both the mentor and the mentoree have a clear understanding of what their new partnership will look like and what it will achieve, then each party can receive optimal benefits from the mentorship experience. A responsible first step to all such arrangements is to resolve questions that have the potential to derail what most people start out knowing is God's will. Once these have been answered and the majority of differences have been worked out, the prospects of the mentor and the mentoree, being enriched by the relationship, are greatly improved. As more and more officers are being groomed to take the reins of their predecessors, successful mentorships become vital to lasting fruit that endures so God's vision of potent kingdom effectiveness through His five-fold ministry staff can be actuated.

Glossary of Key Terms

Administration

The process of managing and disposing of clerical, ministerial, political and other details.

Agent, Agencies

A person that transacts business for another in a distant location.

Ambassadorial

What pertains to an ambassador or what comes from a representative sent to a foreign land.

Ancient

From a very old period in history. Archaic, primeval, before counting eras.

Angels

A heavenly messenger.

Anointing

A special call by a higher power or authority to serve others in its behalf. Signified sometimes by the pouring of oil upon the head to consecrate.

Apocalypse

A natural event brought on by spiritual, heavenly, or celestial sources that occurs because it was foreteold.

Apostle

A specially commissioned messenger sent by a deity, temple, or government with a message that performs

miraculous signs and wonders.

Apostleship

The embassadorial activities of an apostle and his or her embassy site.

Assignment

A delegated task of duty short or long term in duration.

Authorities

People in positions that possess or give power to act in another's stead to enforce obedienc and alter or restrain conduct and behavior.

Authority

The lawful right to impose law, enforce obedience and overall command specific behavior and conduct.

Authorize

Delegated license, power, privilige or act in an official capacity.

Bible

General word for book. Traditionally applied to a sacred book, specifically that containing the inspired word of Creator God.

Biblical Order

Ecclesiastical structure, hierarchy, policy and government based upon the Bible, see above.

Canon Law

Law and government founded upon the word of God as ecclesiastically translated by the leaders of the New Testament church. Canon comes from the Greek, Kanon, referring to the New Creation in Jesus Christ and all that pertains to or emanates from it.

Chrio

A type of anointing, specifically that applied to Christian ministers to enable and empower their divine service.

Chrisma

The internally applied anointing dispensed by the Holy Spirit that makes one a child of Creator God.

Christ

The Messianic name of Jesus the Son of the Most High God. Means anointed, as in Messiah. The ah at the end of the name refers to the Lord, making His title specifically identify Him as the anointed Lord.

Church Leaders

Generally encompassing the offices of 1 Corinthians 12:28,29 and Ephesians 4:11, the term applies to those entrusted by Christ with the oversight of His ecclesia.

Commission

An official task delegated to one dispatched away from the sender to accomplish. Usually accompanied by special signs and authority to prohibit the commission from being opposed.

Constitution

The formal document drafted by entity founders that legitimizes its right to exist and forms the basis of its order, structure, government and authority.

Counsel

Wisdom, guidance, and instruction given to another in the form of advice, direction and insight.

Deity

Another name for a god or divine, heavenly, or celestial being.

Delegated

Assignment of a task, commission, or project by one in authority that is initially responsible for them, to another to handle on his or her behalf.

Dispatch

To send forth on a mission, journey, task, or commission to accomplish express duties or to execute determined orders.

Dispensation

A form of the word dispense, refers to God's outpouring and its economic and managerial requirement at an appointed time or under particular circumstances.

Divine

Celestial, spiritual, eternal.

Divine Order

The order and arrangement of God's business and entitites according to His preordained plans and designs. *See Biblical Order.*

Divine Person

A personified expression of a supernatural, eternal, or otherworldly being. Jesus Christ and Melchizedek are examples of.

Dunamis

Another word for miracles and the distinct supernatural abilities, knowledge, skill and wisdom that understands and performs them.

Dunamite

The name given in this book for the official Miracle Worker identified in 1 Corinthians 12:28,29.

Duties

The responsibilities, actions, tasks and assignments that are required by those placed in an office to authorize their actions on behalf of another.

Eden

Also called paradise, it is symbolically called by Bible prophets as God's garden. It is where the first man and woman lived.

Elisha

Elijah's protégé and successor.

Embassy

A word used for an ambassador's office, the ambassador and the people and property assigned to administrate a country's affairs in a foreign land. One synonym for an embassy is satellite.

Eternal

That which has no beginning and cannot end.

Evangelist

Third member of the Ephesians 4:11 staff.

Functionary

One that carries out the functions of another or on someone else's behalf.

Gift

A present in the form of an object, or the talents and aptitudes one receives from the Creator at birth to support their life, and propel their destinies.

Govern

To administrate the laws, regulations and policies a founder or superior impose on the entity over which he or she is assigned; often delegated.

Great Apostle

Jesus Christ, according to Hebrews 3:1.

Hand

Symbolically in this book, the five fold ministry as the operative hand of God in Christ.

Holy Spirit

The third member of creation's Godhead, comprised of God the Father, His Son Jesus, and His

Eternal Spirit.

Humanist

What Paul the apostle refers to as the commandments and doctrines of men as spawned by seducing spirits and doctrines of devils, in 1 Timothy.

Imagery

Picture representations of ideas, feelings, beliefs, signs and symbols.

Immortal

That which cannot die (that is, return to the dust).

Institution

The formal organization of a body, class or group as held together by its prescribed order, consitution, and government all designed for its prosperous perpetuity.

Intercession

The acts, words, prayers, and processes employed by one on behalf of another that is weaker, unauthorized, underprivileged in need of favor and mercy with an authorityable to relieve their distress.

Jesus

Creator God's first begotten Son, Savior and Redeemer, and second member of the Godhead.

Kanon

Greek word for the New Creation born of God's Spirit, its sphere of existence and the eternal law that governs it, as well as the sphere of the apostle's ministry and authorty. **See Canon.**

Kingdom

The territorial sphere and realm of a monarch, a king, as its sole ruler.

Leadership

The institution of leaders that execute a plan, fulfill a vision, carry out a mission or commission through others on behalf of a visionary, authority, or founder.

Lucifer

Satan's pre-damnation name when he served the Most High as a covering cherub.

Magical

That which pertains to magic, that is the illusions, deceptions, and manipulations of a priest (Magi) of a fallen being.

Mantle

Spiritually, a term for the invisible covering (ministry uniform) worn by a servant of a deity. Elisha took on Elijah's to symbolize his induction into Yahweh's service and his assumption of the prophetic duties, powers, license, and stature his predecessor vacated upon being translated to heaven. Remaining in the earth, it later fell to John the Baptists.

Melakim

The messenger insitution of ancient Israel that pretypifies the Ephesians 4:11 offices.

Melchizedek

Founder and holder of the office of Creator God's eternal priesthood into which all New Creation members of Christ's body belong, and over which He was installed as High Priest. Occupied pre-Jebusite and Davidic Jerusalem until Abraham's covenant was ratified.

Mentor

A skilled professional or veteran in a certain field that guides, aids, and equips for success another rising in his or her field.

Mentoree

One who is mentored.

Mentorship

The arrangement between a mentor and mentoree.

Messenger

One sent on an errand or assignment to voice the will, thoughts, and actions or intents of another. Official messengers were thusly authorized to perform the assignment or otherwise act out the message in the sender's stead.

Minister

One that serves another in an official capacity; a representative that transacts business or mediates the affairs of a government, country, court, palace, or temple.

Ministry

The diverse services and activities of one installed as a minister. The process of

managing and disposing of clerical, ministerial, political and other details.

Miracle

An event or sign that betokens a divine action or serves to warn c confirm humans of a divine presence or future involvement i their affairs.

Moses

Israel's 5th generation prophet, although he fits more the category of an Old Testament apostle. Moses as Israel's first deliverer, instituted its government and founded it as a country for its perpetual calling as Creator God's only nation.

Natural Signs

Supernatural events that show themselves in acts of nature or human behavior and conduct.

New Testament

A name for the New Covenant o Jesus Christ that birthed His New Creation race of redeemed souls.

Officer

One that ocupies an office.

Officials

Authorized agents or representatives of a principal.

Old Testament

The Mosiac covenant the Lord made with Israel that consisted o its laws, regulations, government and priesthood.

Pala'

Hebrew word for sign, the Greek semeion.

Pastor

The 4th member of the Ephesians 4:11 offices.

Powers

People and agencies that exert force or exercise strength and authority in various affairs or upon others.

Priest

A little stronger than the word minister, a priest is the specific servant representative of a deity appointed to mediate between the god and his or her people.

Priesthood

An order of priests. The Bible's are 1st Melchizedek, 2nd Levitical under Aaron, also called the Aaronic Priesthood, 3rd the New Creation priesthood according to Melchizedek's order under Jesus Christ.

Prophecy

A message (dramatized or enacted) from the mouth of a god.

Prophet

A spokesperson for a divine being. Also called nabi which meaning inludes "he who invokes the gods."

Protocol

Entirely action and initiative based, these are the rules, practices, etiquette, behaviors response codes, or reaction guidelines peculiar to a particular group. They regulate its conduct, manage its operations, and order its procedures.

Religion

An organized means of contacting, covenanting with, appeasing and overall relating to a deity or revered person or pursuit. Normally consists of prayers, sacrifices, offerings, devotion, worship, service, and obedience.

Revelation

A truth unveiled for human witness and understanding.

Satellite

In addition to be an orbiting planet, defines a prince's attache in a distant or remote site, a client state dependent upon a more powerful country, what may be considered as a colonial province or a pioneer territorial settlement.

Scripture

The sum of God's words as recorded in the Holy Spirit.

Service Classifications

A term used in this book to explain the different groups and duties of the individual offices of the five fold.

Sign

Biblically and spiritually speaking, an event, symbol, divine or natural action that betokens a divine intent or sentiment. May appear as a drama, image, miracle or disaster.

Skill

A special ability perfected by practice, repetition, experience, and training that renders a person competent in a given area.

Soul

The second sphere, immaterial side, of the human make up that stores it content from the spirit compulsively; the mind's receipt of external stimuli.

Sovereign

Rendered Almighty God's preemptive right to intervene in human affairs as Creator.

Spiritual

That which is otherworldly, immortal and immaterial, heavenly and/or eternal.

Spirituality

Having the origin, nature or quality of the invisible, divine and/or celestial.

Station

The ranking position of a person within a class or group.

Ten Decalogues

Another word for Ten Commandments.

Teras

Greek word for sign.

The Five Fold

A colloquial term for the Ephesians 4:11 posts of apostle, prophet, evangelist, pastor and teacher.

The Spirit

Generally a term for any supernatural action or initiative, usually refers to the Holy Spirit.

The Teacher

Fifth office of Ephesians 4:11, although the 3rd one in the line of 1 Corinthians 12:28, 29.

Theology

The verbiage and supposed logic of God. Typically refers to any body of knowledge addressing deities.

Tithe

Bible word for tenth. Also called firstfruits, increase, the tithe is returned to God as Creator as His earned portion for supplying earth's provisions a acquisitions.

Truth

What conforms to creation and it design, laws, and government as upheld by the Creator's invisible agents and agencies.

Wisdom

Empowering knowledge rendered fruitful by understanding that when acted upon produces, elevates, enriches, and prospers

Wonder

A prodigy, omen, token, sign.

Yad

"Hand" (Hebrew); meaning includes ministry.

Table of Sources & References

Dictionary of Christian Lore & Legend

JCJ Medford

Thames & Hudson, LTD, London 1983

The Original Roget's Thesaurus of English Words & Phrases, New Edition

Revised by Robert A Dutch, O.B.E.,

St. Martins Press, New York, 1879, 1936, 1962, USA 1965

Zondervan Compact Bible Dictionary

Zondervan, Grand Rapids, 1993

Random House Webster Collegiate Dictionary

By Random House, Inc. 1995, 1992, 1991

The Barnhart Concise Dictionary of Etymology; The Origins of American English Words

Robert Barnhart

B. H. Wilson Company, 1995

The World Before and After Jesus: Desire of the Everlasting Hills &

Civilization and the Gift of the Jews

Thomas Cahill

Nan S. Talese, Anchor Books, New York , 1994, 2001

A Reader's Guide to the Great Religions

Edited by Charles J Adams

The Free Press, A Division of the Macmillan Company 1965

The Harvard Business Essentials: Coaching & Mentoring

Harvard Business School, Publishing Corp. 2004

People Skills

Robert Bolton, Ph.D.

Simon & Schuster, Inc. 1979

A Latin Dictionary, Freunds Latin Dictionary

Charlton T Lewis, Ph. D. & Charles Short, LL. D.

Oxford at the Clarendon Press, 1966

International Standard Bible Encyclopedia

Electronic Database copyright 1996, Biblesoft

The New Ungers Bible Dictionary

Moody Press of Chicago, Illinois, 1988

Merriam Webster's Collegiate Dictionary 10th Edition, 1994

Merriam Webster's, Incorporated, Springfield, Massachusetts USA

The Dictionary of Classical Mythology, Religion, Literature, and Art

Oskar Seyffert 1841-1906

Revised and Edited by Henry Nettleship and J. E. Sandys

Gramercy Books, Distributed by Random House Value Publishing, Inc., New Jersey 1995

Index

Administration 21, 22, 82, 83

Agencies 15, 151

Agents 15, 16, 19, 53, 59, 60, 84, 94, 114, 125, 127, 130

Ambassadorial 15, 41

Ancient 125, 126

Angels 125

Anointing 82, 103, 113, 114, 115, 116, 117, 118, 119, 120, 121, 135, 136

Apocalypse 35

Apostle 6, 7, 9, 10, 12, 16, 24, 25, 30, 31, 32, 35, 43, 50, 51, 52, 54, 55, 61, 72, 80, 86, 91, 94, 99, 101, 102, 108, 110, 111, 116, 141

Apostles 128

Apostles and Prophets 5, 6, 7, 8, 11, 13, 25, 110

Apostleship 9, 11, 40, 50, 58, 91, 99, 103, 117, 128, 151

Assignment 15, 18, 28, 39, 41, 60, 78, 81, 99, 114, 120

Authorities 14, 15, 16, 27, 53, 54, 55, 56, 93, 95, 128, 153

Authority 10, 13, 14, 15, 16, 18, 19, 20, 23, 24, 25, 26, 32, 33, 34, 37, 38, 40, 49, 50, 51, 52, 53, 54, 57, 59, 60, 73, 76, 79, 80, 82, 83, 88, 91, 93, 94, 95, 96, 97, 98, 109, 118, 120, 121, 124, 125, 127, 130, 133, 135, 136, 139, 140, 141, 142, 144, 145, 154

Authorize 14, 15, 17

Bible iii

Biblical Order 7

Canon Law 33

Chrio 118, 121

Chrisma 114, 115, 119, 120, 121

Christ 129

Church Leaders 5, 13, 25, 27, 41

Commission 7, 14, 15, 18, 19, 39, 60, 82, 83, 116

Constitution 33, 34, 77

Counsel 10, 25, 39, 48, 66, 98, 132, 135, 136, 154

Courts 15, 27, 84, 93, 94, 95

Deity 23, 31, 40, 93, 95, 96, 97, 116, 117, 147, 148

Delegated 14, 16, 18, 19, 23, 25, 32, 39, 53, 60, 76, 93, 95, 97, 128

Delegatory 19

Dispatch 14, 15, 16, 31, 48, 83, 124

Dispensation 67, 115, 116, 117, 126, 128

Divine 5, 6, 7, 10, 11, 13, 18, 23, 24, 25, 27, 30, 32, 33, 35, 37, 38, 39, 40, 43, 46, 50, 52, 53, 54, 55, 63, 74, 75, 76, 77, 79, 83, 89, 91, 92, 93, 94, 95, 96, 97, 102, 111, 114, 115, 117, 121, 124, 125, 127, 128, 129, 146, 147

Divine Order 5, 6, 11, 13, 27, 30, 33, 50, 52, 53, 75, 111

Divine Person   124

Dunamis   123

Duties 18, 19, 23, 26, 52, 61,
76, 79, 80, 81, 83, 92, 94,
95, 105, 117, 119, 149, 153

Eden   19, 66, 70, 87

Elijah   11, 126, 128

Elisha   11, 126, 128

Eternal 9, 10, 14, 16, 17, 24,
27, 31, 35, 36, 42, 52, 54,
55, 56, 57, 60, 63, 65, 66,
69, 70, 71, 73, 75, 82, 84,
92, 98, 105, 109, 111, 116,
120, 129, 147, 148

Evangelical 5, 10, 13, 25, 30,
45

Evangelist 5, 6, 9, 10, 12, 31,
51, 61, 80, 91, 101, 108,
110, 112, 128

Functionary 18, 60, 91, 93, 98

Gifts 8, 9, 22, 23, 25, 31, 38,
39, 41, 49, 50, 52, 53, 71,
72, 73, 74, 75, 79, 80, 88,
89, 100, 104, 111, 112, 114,
117, 134

Godhead   19, 21, 25, 34, 36

Govern 10, 20, 32, 34, 88, 136

Great Apostle   19

Hand 8, 10, 12, 24, 31, 32, 40,
51, 63, 67, 80, 90, 97, 102,
103, 107, 122, 125, 127,
140, 141, 144, 153

Highway   126

Holy Spirit 15, 16, 17, 24, 28,
31, 34, 38, 41, 43, 48, 57,
68, 77, 108, 114, 115, 117,

120, 121, 127, 128, 134,
143, 151

Humanist 5, 28, 66, 67, 85

Imagery   125

Immortal 16, 17, 23, 27, 35,
87, 129, 147

Influence 14, 17, 18, 20, 27,
44, 51, 53, 80, 91, 94, 98,
101, 102, 133, 135, 136,
139, 140, 142, 144, 145,
153, 154

Institution 6, 10, 11, 20, 21,
22, 23, 26, 33, 37, 48, 55,
58, 60, 61, 76, 153

Intercession   48

Jesus   124

Joshua   11, 97, 103

Kanon   10

Kingdom 6, 7, 9, 10, 19, 33,
37, 38, 41, 44, 51, 55, 57,
59, 61, 62, 63, 65, 73, 83,
87, 91, 94, 99, 104, 105,
107, 111, 114, 120, 121,
127, 128, 153

Leadership 10, 13, 14, 25, 26,
27, 28, 48, 53, 72, 80, 84,
86, 90, 103, 110, 135, 144

Lucifer   35

Magical   32

Magicians   31, 32

Mantle 6, 7, 10, 16, 51, 109,
118, 130, 135, 136

Mantles 7, 10, 11, 76, 140

Melakim   60, 61, 80

Melchizedek   9

Mentor   132, 133, 138, 143, 145, 156, 158, 159, 160

Mentoree   138, 158, 159

Mentorship   132, 133, 135, 136, 138, 150, 155, 156, 157, 158, 159, 160

Messengers   126

Messiah   18, 32, 55, 126, 129

Ministers   1, 5, 6, 7, 8, 11, 12, 13, 18, 20, 24, 25, 27, 28, 33, 37, 38, 39, 40, 43, 45, 49, 50, 51, 52, 53, 54, 55, 60, 61, 66, 67, 71, 74, 75, 78, 79, 83, 85, 91, 92, 93, 94, 96, 99, 102, 104, 108, 110, 111, 112, 113, 114, 115, 117, 119, 120, 121, 128, 130, 132, 133, 136, 137, 138, 140, 141, 142, 143, 144, 147, 149, 152, 153

Ministries   5, 6, 7, 9, 12, 16, 25, 27, 28, 31, 32, 33, 38, 39, 42, 45, 48, 52, 53, 55, 67, 74, 75, 90, 93, 97, 109, 128, 140, 141, 144

Ministry   6, 8, 9, 10, 12, 13, 14, 19, 20, 26, 28, 31, 32, 33, 37, 38, 39, 40, 41, 42, 44, 45, 48, 49, 50, 51, 52, 53, 55, 59, 60, 61, 62, 66, 73, 74, 75, 76, 78, 79, 80, 81, 82, 83, 85, 90, 91, 92, 93, 94, 96, 99, 100, 101, 102, 110, 113, 114, 115, 116, 117, 118, 120, 121, 124, 130, 132, 133, 134, 135, 136, 141, 142, 143, 144, 150, 151, 152, 153, 154

Miracle   128, 129

Miracles   9, 15, 51, 119, 121, 123, 124, 126, 127, 128, 129

Miraculous   126

Miraculous Power   128

Mopheth   129

Moses'   10, 11, 15, 34, 35, 109, 124, 128, 147, 148

Natural Signs   126

Natural World   18, 68, 127

Nature   124, 125

New Testament 1, 2, 5, 10, 16, 24, 27, 29, 30, 31, 32, 33, 39, 40, 41, 60, 61, 64, 66, 72, 77, 79, 82, 98, 99, 113, 123, 126, 127, 129, 130, 131, 147, 148

Officer   5, 11, 14, 15, 18, 20, 28, 40, 59, 75, 76, 78, 79, 80, 82, 83, 84, 90, 94, 100, 102, 104, 108, 110, 112

Officers 5, 6, 8, 10, 14, 15, 20, 21, 23, 27, 28, 30, 31, 33, 37, 41, 42, 58, 59, 60, 65, 66, 67, 73, 74, 75, 76, 78, 80, 83, 86, 90, 94, 100, 101, 108, 109, 117

Officials 16, 18, 20, 22, 24, 27, 33, 50, 60, 71, 73, 75, 84, 105, 130

Old Testament   9, 11, 12, 31, 32, 60, 61, 72, 107, 121, 123, 126, 129, 147

Pala'   129

Pastor   5, 6, 7, 9, 10, 11, 13, 17, 18, 43, 61, 91, 101, 102, 108, 109, 110, 141

Powers 15, 18, 19, 34, 40, 41, 53, 54, 73, 79, 86, 93, 97, 116, 117, 125, 126, 127, 128, 130

Priest 60, 94, 96, 97, 121, 146, 147, 148, 149, 150

Priesthood 9, 16, 22, 96, 146, 147, 148

Prophecy 9, 61, 71, 72, 86, 102, 108, 109, 125, 126, 129

Prophet 6, 7, 9, 11, 25, 26, 43, 50, 54, 60, 61, 63, 80, 91, 101, 102, 108, 109, 110, 111, 128, 146

Prophetic Link 125

Protocol 15, 21, 146, 152

Religion 128

Revelation 124

Scripture 5, 6, 7, 8, 9, 10, 12, 17, 21, 23, 24, 28, 31, 33, 36, 49, 50, 52, 54, 55, 74, 86, 98, 99, 102, 104, 105, 121, 124, 126, 131, 149

Scripture 126

Service Classifications 18

Signs 125, 126, 129

Signs and Wonders 9, 115, 123, 128, 129

Skills 23, 81

Soul 17, 22, 26, 34, 36, 69, 71, 110, 111

Sovereign 5, 18, 31, 33, 82, 93, 94

Spiritual 125

Spirituality 15, 141

Station 18, 19, 55

Ten Decalogues 34

Teras 123, 129

The Five Fold 5, 6, 8, 9, 20, 27, 53, 73, 84

The Spirit 5, 15, 48, 91, 111, 117, 118, 123, 126, 134

The Teacher 1, 5, 7, 9, 10, 11, 61, 80, 110, 111, 112

Theology 8, 10, 20, 49, 102

Tithe 133, 145, 146, 147, 148, 149, 150, 151, 152, 153

Titles 9, 12, 13, 14, 16, 18, 19, 20, 23, 24, 25, 26, 27, 61, 65, 74, 82, 92, 100, 108

Truth 128

Voice 124, 125

Wisdom 5, 8, 10, 21, 25, 27, 28, 29, 31, 32, 38, 41, 47, 48, 49, 51, 52, 53, 54, 56, 58, 60, 62, 63, 64, 65, 66, 73, 74, 75, 83, 89, 97, 102, 104, 116, 118, 119, 121, 127, 133, 135, 136, 139, 149, 154

Wonders 124, 128

Yad 10, 31

About the Author

Paula A. Price is vastly becoming the international voice on the subject of apostolic and prophetic ministry. She is widely recognized as a modern-day apostle with a potent prophetic anointing. Having been in active full-time ministry since 1985, she has founded and established three churches, an apostolic and prophetic Bible institute, a publication company, consulting firm, and global collaborative network linking apostles and prophets together for the purpose of kingdom vision and ventures. With an international itinerant ministry she has transformed the lives of many through her wisdom and revelation of God's kingdom.

As a former sales and marketing executive, Paula blends ministerial and entrepreneurial applications in her ministry to enrich and empower a diverse audience with the skills and abilities to take kingdoms for the Lord Jesus Christ. A lecturer, teacher, curriculum developer and business trainer, she globally consults Christian businesses, churches, schools and assemblies. She has over a 20-year period developed a superior curriculum to effectively train Christian ministers and professionals, particularly the apostle and the prophet. Her programs often are used in both secular and non-secular environments worldwide. Although she has written over 25 books, manuals, and other course material on the apostolic and prophetic, she is most recognized for her unique 1,600-term *Prophets' Dictionary,* a concise prophetic training manual entitled *Church Prophets*, and her most recent release, *Eternity's Generals*, an explanation of today's apostle.

Beyond the pulpit, Paula is the provocative talk show host of her own program, *Let's Just Talk: Where God Makes Sense.* She brings the pulpit to the pew, weekly applying God's wisdom and divine pragmatism to today's world solutions. Her ministry goal is to make Christ's teachings and churches relevant for today. "Eternity in the Now" is the credo through which she accomplishes it.

In addition to her vast experience, Paula has a D.Min. and a Ph.D. in Religious Education from Word of Truth Seminary in Alabama. She is also a wife, mother of three daughters, and the grandmother of two. She and her husband Tom presently pastor New Creation Worship Assembly in Tulsa, OK.

Other Works by Dr. Paula A. Price

♦ *The Prophets' Dictionary: The Ultimate Guide to Supernatural Wisdom*

♦ *Church Prophets: A Powerful Five-Fold Tool for Church Leaders*

♦ *Prophecy: God's Divine Communications Media*

♦ *Eternity's Generals: The Wisdom of Apostleship*

For additional copies of this book or other works by this author, call 918-446-5542 or visit our website at www.drpaulaprice.com.

CPSIA information can be obtained
at www.ICGtesting.com
Printed in the USA
LVHW110412141021
700395LV00009B/534